Ready, Fire, Aim

HOW A SUCCESSFUL SILICON VALLEY
EXECUTIVE DISCOVERED THE INFLUENCE OF GOD IN
HIS LIFE

Paul C Ely

Palo Alto, California

All Scriptures unless otherwise noted, are taken from the *Holy Bible, New International Version*, Copyright© 1973, 1978, 1984 by International Bible Society. Used by permission of Zondervan. All rights reserved.

Book Layout ©2013 BookDesignTemplates.com

Ready, Fire, Aim/Paul C. Ely

ISBN 10:1493751352
ISBN 13: 978-1493751358

Table of Contents

Acknowledgments:

This book would not have come into existence were it not for my sister Frances Ely Bostwick and my wife Geri. I give my heartfelt thanks to them both for the enormous help provided during the long process of getting this book into print.

My sister spent many hours editing my awkward phrasing, grammar and punctuation. She reviewed my writing, critiqued the content and rewrote paragraphs from time to time. Fran edited and rewrote much of Part 1 to be more concise. We had face-to-face meetings numerous times to work on the book either in Colorado where she lives or here in California. I would also like to recognize the patience, tolerance and help of Bob Bostwick, my brother-in-law, as my sister and I discussed endlessly some part of the book. We depended on his good judgment to move us forward.

Geri and I share an office in our home so she could literally look over my shoulder as I wrote. Geri provided quick feedback and guidance throughout. She knew the story well and I relied on her judgment. I do not come naturally to writing and when motivation was needed Geri provided it. The encouragement and guidance from these two ladies brought this book to fruition.

Introduction

This project all started a few years ago when my two sons said to me, "Dad, you've given us much good advice over the years. Would you just write down those lessons so it will be there for your grandchildren?" Each of my sons has two daughters whom I love dearly, so this sounded like a reasonable request. Little did I know what that project would grow into!

I started compiling a list of some of the things I had learned that had been helpful in guiding my life. As time passed I kept adding to the list and came to realize that some of these were issues of morality and ethics, some were practical guidelines of how to live, and many were tips on how to be productive and successful in one's life and career.

It became clear that, along with lessons from my parents, much of what I wanted to pass to my grandchildren I had learned during my years at Hewlett Packard. I always said that my time at HP had improved my character—made me a better person. That may seem like a strange comment to make about a for-profit organization, but HP was a very special company, and my quarter century there was at the right time in the company's development. Bill Hewlett and Dave Packard, the company's founders, were extraordinary people and I had the opportunity to learn from them.

This gradually expanding list of lessons was quite a mixed bag. Many of the items had stories associated with them, and these stories were often necessary to properly understand the lesson and its value. The list morphed into a book about my life and

1

career. My sister became aware of the project and offered to help. She had been an English major at Northwestern University and wrote frequently in her career.

But then, at the age of seventy-six, an extraordinary event turned my life inside out, and has changed my entire perspective on this project and everything else in my life. Let me explain.

Early in the morning on April 15, 2008, I was lying in bed thinking over my plans for the day as I normally do before getting up. This, of course, was tax day and also the day of Pope Benedict's visit, none of which seemed to have anything to do with what happened next. As I lay there, quite suddenly an overwhelming feeling of intense gratitude and thankfulness for the good fortune that had filled my life flowed over me. The intensity and depth of this experience is well beyond my limited ability to describe or relate. It continued, as I saw my entire life flashing before me like a YouTube video.

I saw my childhood and my wonderful parents who guided me so well in a home filled with laughter and security in spite of the Great Depression and the Second World War. I relived my undergraduate college days and the fun and friendships balanced with my much-enjoyed but intense studies in engineering physics. I saw my first date with Barbara Sheiry, then our marriage, the start of our life together, the birth of our two sons and my first years as an engineer. Then came our move to California and my years at Hewlett Packard where I learned so much and experienced almost unbelievable success. I had started as an R and D engineer and twenty years later, I was an executive vice-president responsible for more than half of a multi-billion-dollar company.

I'm not sure how long this "video" took, possibly only seconds, but it was fully detailed. At the end came an amazing realization— *it had been God working in my life that had created my success and life of good fortune*. It was not my skill, capability, or initiative; it had been God. This realization was implanted permanently. I had no doubt. Then I heard the message: *"Paul, you must find God."*

This event affected me profoundly. It altered my life in every possible way. The final section of this book tells about my search for God and where that trail leads me. What happened that April and the changed life that followed brought forth a new perspective on the events throughout my life and a changed purpose for this book. We worked on the book as my new life was unfolding. By the time my new perspective developed the writing was well along.

The next step was to go back over the story and identify where there were providential events. Throughout my HP career I felt I was experiencing an extraordinary string of good luck. (Many at HP probably have felt that way about me.) Now I know it was neither good luck nor my great skill.

Identifying these providential events by their nature was quite subjective. In a few instances there was no question that something very unusual and quite difficult to explain was going on. While I was going back over the draft identifying these events, often I came to a new and deeper understanding of my life experiences. These providential events are marked and/or commented on in the book (see list of such events with page numbers in the Caption Table at the end of the book).

The title of this story, *Ready, Fire, Aim*, requires an explanation. At HP's annual management meetings it was a tradition for the executives to be actors in a skit intended to provoke laughter from the audience. The script for the skit made fun of each executive actor's foibles or habitual behavior. One year the script had me repeatedly mouthing the phrase, "ready, fire, aim," in my neither soft nor dulcet tone. My coworkers loved it and the saying became a favorite way for all to use in humorously chiding me. You can be sure it was worked into the skit from then on.

Unfortunately (or fortunately) this description of my behavior was accurate. It suggested I was "shooting from the hip," making decisions very quickly. To help myself feel better I justified my behavior as coping with the rapid rate of change in the computer business. I claimed it was analogous to the British invention of tracer bullets during the Second World War to enhance their aim in shooting down fast-moving German planes. Ready, Fire, Aim was the protocol I followed—act quickly, then refine the results.

It appears now that this phrase, "ready, fire, aim," was more appropriate for this book than it might seem. In fact, it does represent God's plan for my life. He devoted thirty years making me Ready, then Fired me forward by sending me to Hewlett Packard for an incredible career, and finally, gave me new Aim and purpose at an age when most men think only of the couch or possibly a game of golf. In reviewing my writing the deeper understanding mentioned earlier has caused me to realize that there came a point when it appears I made a choice that diverted me from God's plan for my training. Had I not done so there might have been a different ending to this story. Fortunately, He did not give up on me entirely but it was many years before He awakened me to His presence. More about that as the story unfolds.

PART I — READY

Preparing for Career and Life

I was made READY for my adult life and career through my upbringing. My childhood, the love and support of my parents, the good examples of grandparents, the education I received right through college, and the wholesome experiences I participated in as I matured impacted the life choices I made as I pursued my career with Hewlett Packard. My father had an important and pronounced impact on my life and on the man I was to become. He would be pleased to know that. When I had some important decisions to make that changed the course of my life, my upbringing helped prepare me. I was READY for the challenges that lay ahead.

CHAPTER 1

Family and Lessons for Life

Right From the Start

Upon reflection, I believe I was destined to be an engineer. Right from the beginning, I was fascinated by all things mechanical and electrical. I remember taking things apart and putting them back together—much to my mother's frustration. I had wires strung across my bedroom to catch my younger sister and her snooping. Generally, it all worked.

One of my earliest memories was accompanying my grandfather, Louis X. Ely, to a foundry he owned and managed in Monessen, Pennsylvania. He made castings for machine tools. I stood there watching workers pour molten metal into molds. My grandfather was obviously pleased that I was interested in mechanical things and manufacturing. I may not have realized it at the time, but the process I was witnessing and my grandfather's expertise and leadership skills inspired me.

His son, my father, Paul C. Ely, had a major influence on my interest in engineering. He was a graduate of Lehigh University with a degree in engineering metallurgy (working with metals). He spent all of his work life with U. S. Steel Corporation, except during the Depression when he was laid off. His career took him from being an engineering intern in McKeesport, Pennsylvania to being the Vice President of Tubular Operations at the U. S. Steel headquarters in Pittsburgh.

When I was still a kid, Dad developed a machine that galvanized steel pipe automatically. It pulled a long piece of pipe through a big tub with galvanizing solution. I watched as he made a model and I remember that the entire process stirred my technical interest.

Dad took me into the steel plant to show me the galvanizing mill when his invention first went into operation. Then he went out of his way to show me the machine that straightened the long lengths of pipe before they were galvanized. This machine used grooved rollers to bend the pipe just the right amount in every direction. Honestly, it looked like a writhing snake as it went through. And, voila, out the other end came a straight piece of pipe. How could bending a pipe make it straight? He told me to figure that out! I thought about that enigma many times in later life.

Hobbies help

Many of Dad's hobbies involved building mechanical and electrical things. When I was a kid living in McKeesport, my dad started building model railroads. Not the typical Lionel trains but the larger H-gauge models. He patiently constructed the train cars, the tracks and the buildings, sometimes from scratch. He would start with kits for the cars but he would change the design and make the pieces for the cars himself. To create the track, Dad brought home thin pieces of steel. Then he would cut little pieces of wood to make the ties. He would cut all the pieces just the right size to make the curves and put tiny spikes in like you see on a real railroad line. I could hardly believe my dad had built such an incredible model true in every detail to a real working railroad. I was allowed to run the trains from the control panel with his supervision. The train was set up at Christmas and ran all around the living room of our home. My mom was a good sport about all this.

My favorite courses in school were science and math. These interests extended to my hobbies as a child. I became very interested in putting together radios and fussing with electronics. I had a basement workshop jammed with old radios and other gadgets I had rescued from scrap heaps of every radio store in town. I would make the rounds on my bicycle. The shop owners all knew me and would save odds and ends of old radios. Keep in mind this was during the 1940s so radios were a major source of news and communication. Along with this, I devoured my favorite magazines—*Popular Mechanics* and *Scientific American*.

All in the Family

My family was central as I was growing up and it was through them that I learned my values and many lessons that influenced my life. Mom (Jean Lillian Campbell) and Dad were married in May 1931 in McKeesport. Dad was working at National Tube and Mom was ready to settle down and raise a family. Then disaster struck! The Depression went into full swing and my dad was laid off. At this time, my mom realized she was pregnant and they could not afford the lease on their little apartment. So, they moved in with Mom's parents, William and Anna Campbell. My mother's sister, Frances, was still living at home. It was a crowded household full of love, support, and laughter.

My dad took any odd job he could find to earn some money during those Depression years. He even took a job as a steward with United Airlines helping passengers climb in and out over the wing of a small plane that carried six passengers. We lived very simply and frugally and made do with what little we had. I recall several occasions when out-of-luck men would come to the back door and my grandmother gave them food or a little money to help them out. There was always enough to help others.

In 1935, my father was rehired at the steel plant and times were better. My parents designed and built a home in a nice neighborhood where there were other kids to play with. I loved those years. We played sandlot tackle football on a rocky field across the street and kick the can on the street in front of our house. In the winter we sledded down the hill across a creek and into a spacious meadow.

A hard-fought lesson

I remember one winter our neighbor flooded his backyard to create an ice-skating rink. A kid named Billy was usually there. He was a real bully and I was often one of his victims. He would grab my hat and hide it from me. I vividly recall coming home one day crying and telling my parents that Billy took my hat and I didn't want to go over there anymore. With that, my father pushed me out the door and said, "You go back there and get your hat. Fight him if you have to. But you can't come back here until you have your hat." I then realized my parents were not going to fight my battles for me. Well, back I went! I fought the guy and got my hat. And I never had a problem with him again. I couldn't believe it!

What a lesson: you are responsible for your own well-being. You can't rely on others to take care of you. Even better, my father believed I could handle it and I did!

The War to End All Wars

On December 7, 1941, Japan attacked Pearl Harbor. Four days later, U. S. Steel sent my father to the National Tube Division in Lorain, Ohio. He and others were given the job of converting the Lorain pipe mill to producing bomb and shell casings. He lived in the steel plant for months. The entire country was committed to the war effort. Every individual did what he or she had to do to further the cause of freedom and win the war.

By that summer, my parents sold their home in McKeesport and rented a house in Lorain. It broke my dad's heart to sell that house. He and Mom had put so much of themselves into it. Lorain was a town of about 75,000 located just west of Cleveland on the shores of Lake Erie. It was a difficult move for us, particularly for my mother and me. Mom had to leave her family, friends of a lifetime, and a quality of life with which she was familiar. I felt awful about leaving my friends. Mom spent her time caring for my sister, Francie, who was two. I eventually made friends in the neighborhood and in the nearby school.

Life during the war was difficult. We had to sacrifice, like eating meager meals with little meat, and use ration stamps to purchase goods. There was little available gas to drive or take trips. Everyone was called upon to make sacrifices, working long hours and making do with little. I even remember seeing, as I drove across the bridge, the women who took jobs in the ship building plant in the harbor where previously only men were working.

I had to rely on my family, my friends at school, and some sports for pleasure. Dad started playing tennis with me and I became obsessed with the game. I would go to the clay courts near Lake Erie early in the morning and help the city workers chalk the lines on the courts. Then I would hang around until some group needed another player. As I became better at the sport, Dad backed off and I was able to pick up games with the better players.

Dad bought a 1941 Buick when the war began, even though he was told he'd never find one because of the war. It was the only car left on the lot; a demo. Once the war started that was it; no more cars were built. I loved that car—it was the smallest Buick made, but it had curved fenders, not square ones. As I grew older and learned to drive I was always pestering Dad about taking the car for a drive. The answer was "Not yet!" I did not get that car until I graduated and was married in 1953. No distractions for me from the challenges I faced in school!

As the war progressed, we listened to the radio every evening before dinner. I was lucky my Dad did not have to leave us to fight. It was hard enough with him in the steel plant so much of the time. But everyone was in the same boat and we were all jubilant when the war finally ended with American victory on two fronts.

Never a dull moment

I always loved sports and looked for opportunities to play whatever game. As I entered high school, I was a small skinny kid. I did not reach my full height until the end of my first year in college. I was not big enough for any of the athletic teams at the school, which were among the best in the state. There was no tennis team so I had to look elsewhere. Then Dad gave me permission to put up a basketball hoop on the detached garage. The driveway had a large concrete pad, which made quite a nice court. After school we would have pickup games frequently with five-man teams. When the school basketball season ended, several of the varsity players would come and join in.

Like many kids my age, I had a paper route. I was probably in eighth grade and I delivered papers every afternoon, usually riding my bike and tossing the papers on people's front porches. There were times in the winter when I would have to trudge through the snow. The experience taught me the importance of being dependable and being good with customers, both important to success in later life.

I was totally bored with a later job of working in a stationery store unpacking boxes and putting items on appropriate shelves. Sometimes I was allowed to drive the truck to deliver items to customers—slightly more interesting.

One summer when I was going into my sophomore year in college, I worked for a construction company that was building a bridge. Reading the blueprints was a natural for me. The foreman looked to me to interpret the plans, and then he would tell the crew what to do. I was physically the smallest guy on the job so there was one task that I was well-suited for and actually enjoyed. When we went to pour cement into the bridge piers, I would stand on the edge of a huge bucket filled with cement that was suspended from a large crane. I held on to the cables attached to the crane, and the crane operator swung me out until the bucket was in position over the form. Then I would slowly release the concrete from the bucket. You can be sure there were few workers who wanted to do that. I enjoyed that summer job. My engineering skills were valuable and riding the bucket certainly wasn't boring!

Another summer, I worked in the steel mill. I loved the steel plant because of the scale of work being done and the excitement of it all. Hot molten metals were combined in huge open-hearth furnaces, baked, and then rolled out and molded into tubes of all sizes, depending on the order. I worked as a clerk in the stockroom, which was not demanding or very interesting. I enjoyed chatting with the steel workers and sometimes would join them for lunch. Other than that, I watched the clock, which never seemed to move. This was an important lesson for me—I did not want to do this kind of work for the rest of my life. Actually, my college grades improved because of this lesson.

Dad: A Loving Taskmaster and Teacher

Dad took me to his alma mater, Lehigh University, the summer before my sophomore year in high school. I was able to tour many interesting labs and, boy, did I find it exciting. After this visit, Lehigh was my choice. However, my parents were concerned that the education I was getting in Lorain was not good enough for me to get into Lehigh.

And so, the summer before my senior year, my parents made arrangements for me to attend University School, a highly rated preparatory school on the east side of Cleveland. In order to get accepted, I had to take a battery of tests and then be interviewed by the headmaster. Then the headmaster met with my parents and told them that my current high school had not prepared me well enough, but the school would admit me if I agreed to attend for two years. My father said he was confident his son would cope with the rigors of University School and, in fact, he guaranteed that I would make straight As during my one year at the school. The headmaster proposed that I could start off as a senior but if I did not do well, then I would have to continue another year.

Later, my Dad told me about his conversation with the headmaster and his confidence that I could get straight As. GULP! Why did Dad do that? As it turned out, his confidence in me was a huge motivator and I did not want to let him down. Guess what? I surprised myself! I did get straight As, an experience that taught me that by committing myself fully, I could accomplish things seemingly beyond my reach. My father was not surprised.

Of course I applied to Lehigh University and was accepted with the help of the grades I got from University School. I talked to Dad about what major I should choose. He advised against studying metallurgy which had been his major. He somehow sensed the technology revolution which was about to take place. I said, "Shouldn't I choose Electrical Engineering as that's where my interests are and the hobbies I most enjoy?" He acknowledged my interests but suggested I study Engineering Physics. He felt that Engineering Physics would better prepare me for the future. It would give me the fundamentals no matter which way the technologies unfolded. I thought about this point and, in the end, did apply for the Engineering Physics degree.

Good Fortune 1: This was profoundly important advice.

This decision set the direction for a career in technology. In ten years, the devices then being taught in Electrical Engineering had ceased to exist. The transistor age took over and then microprocessors, all based on solid-state physics. Because of my education in physics, my career in the rapidly evolving world of technology was greatly enhanced. I relied on that knowledge of physics throughout my career. Surely this was one of the "Defining Moments" in my life.

As Dad was promoted into upper management at the steel plant, one of his biggest challenges was working with the union. My father concluded early on that steel workers were good people and if you treated them fairly, you could make progress. I remember him talking about employees who deserved promotion but were held back because they were minorities. Dad would get a lot of static from workers and even supervisors when he promoted a minority. He felt he was promoting the best person for the job and did not care about his skin color. There was not much discussion about civil rights in those days. Even in places in the North, I remember seeing signs above drinking fountains that indicated "whites only." But Dad held his focus on who could do the job best.

From this I learned that it takes good judgment to know when it is best to "break the rules" and to have the courage to do so.

Dad told me that in his work in the steel plant, he never assigned tasks. Rather than issuing commands, he would tell the workers what was needed and what the goal was and let them work on the solution. He had high expectations for people with whom he worked and he tried to provide them with the tools and opportunities they needed to succeed.

Dinner table discussions

The dinner table in our home was where a large share of my learning took place. It became a tradition for the family to linger around the table sometimes for an hour and discuss the day's events or other important topics. Politics, history, religion, the law, and moral issues were all topics for discussion.

Dad took every opportunity to engage me in discussion on topics he felt were important to me. Often, he challenged me to express my opinion or even to disagree with him. He encouraged me to think things through and develop my own ideas. To the best of my knowledge, none of my friends had experiences like this. Their fathers pretty much lectured them and told them what to do or not do. Dad helped me reason through issues. I did not always reach the point he wanted and we had some lasting disagreements, but often I reasoned my way around to his point of view. Today's young people don't understand that because rarely do their parents even discuss things with them. I learned as much from my sons as they learned from me in the sense that it helped me understand the attitudes of the young people we were hiring at HP.

I learned many lessons about life and people, along with local and world events, from these discussions. Actually, I could write a book on the lessons learned at the dinner table. But for brevity's sake, I will enumerate a few of them to give the reader some sense of the influence my father had on me. Here goes:

- If you don't like a teacher in school, learn to get along with that teacher. You will always have to deal with people you don't like.
- You can't change other people's behavior, only your own response to them.
- Imperfect people can often make important contributions to the decisions and challenges you have in life.
- Everyone should have the opportunity to make mistakes or succeed in life and to learn from that. The true value of a person should be based on how he or she overcomes flaws, deals with challenges and puts skills and talents to good use.
- Don't worry about problems you can't do anything about. Only worry about the things you can resolve.
- Time is a critical factor in almost every decision you make and you must have the judgment and courage to know when to "connect the dots" to make timely decisions. (Sounds like my philosophy of Ready, Fire, Aim. I learned that from my father.)
- There is no such thing as a free lunch. Sounds like a cliché today, but when you seem to be getting something for nothing, look out! It's likely there is some obligation or cost you don't see till it's too late.
- Don't be afraid to question the conventional wisdom when deciding on a course of action. For example, Dad felt the steel industry was a captive of its past, but the top brass did not listen to him. Turns out he was right. So, when people tell you it can't be done, think again and look for ways that it can be done effectively.

Good Fortune 2: Dinner table discussions were a blessing.

What lessons! I cannot underestimate the influence my father had on me as I grew up. He lived and acted in accordance with his beliefs and values. He spent time with me, sometimes playing, sometimes setting high standards for my behavior, sometimes questioning my viewpoints, and many times sharing his perspective on life. He was influencing me in ways I did not truly appreciate at the time. It was as if he and God were partners in shaping the person that I would eventually become. These dinner table lessons have flowed through my life and career. This was the way he behaved as a Dad.

Love, Marriage and Family

I always considered myself somewhat outgoing. I enjoyed and sought out the company of other people. Girls were another thing! I joined in with mixed groups while in high school, mostly with kids who were sons and daughters of family friends. I had a serious relationship with a co-ed from a girl's school when I was at University School. But nothing compared with the relationship that began when I was a junior at Lehigh.

It was a Sunday morning and I was on the cleanup crew after a Saturday night party in our fraternity. The bar was located at the end of the basement under the living room. The only way into it was to stoop down and go through a low door and then down four steps. My roommate brought a friend of his from home to show her the bar and to meet me. In walks this beautiful woman with striking blue eyes and a big smile. Her name was Barbara Sheiry and I was instantly attracted. After we chatted a bit, she left to join her parents. I asked my roommate to get me a date with her.

Obviously, one thing led to another. We thought alike and appreciated each other's sense of humor. Barbara was fun-loving and full of energy, which I found very attractive. She was beautiful with a sense of style and grace. She was a refined woman who did not hesitate to experience adventure. We realized we were in love and in due time talked about marriage.

The marriage took place in the spring of my senior year. After graduation, I took a job with the Sperry Gyroscope Company on Long Island and we settled into life together in Great Neck, NY. On December 28, 1953 our first son, Paul C. Ely III (Skip) was born.

Good Fortune 3: The girl of my dreams and the birth of a son.

Starting a family always provides a new perspective and purpose for life.

Learning From My First Job

It was exciting to start work at Sperry. The group I was assigned to join was designing test equipment to be used with radar systems made for the military. Radar and long-distance telephone used very high frequency radio waves called microwaves. The early years of my career were involved with microwave technology. My first task was to redesign a plug-in for the test equipment to simulate the radar being used. The prior design had not worked but it was a good starting point. I had been working less than a week when I needed to change a few components in the original design. As I did so, a technician accosted me for doing "technician's work". He filed a grievance with their union. That was not a good start!

As time passed I found the highly unionized environment at Sperry very frustrating. Just getting a ten-cent part out of the locked stockroom took a chit signed by a supervisor. Eventually I learned to work around the system and finished my project successfully. I became an expert on this particular test-set and ended up helping the navy techs learn how to test their radar and identify problems. I even went with them on a couple of sixteen-hour flights over the Atlantic on early warning radar planes.

I started taking graduate engineering classes at Brooklyn Polytechnic University. I also learned about the quality of management at Sperry. They seemed weak to me, not very results-oriented, risk adverse, and not sharp technically. At first I thought this would be good since I would stand out among the other engineers. Then it became clear that all levels of management were weak for the most part and could not tell the good guys from the bad guys.

Then things changed for the better. Sperry was establishing a new division in Clearwater, Florida, and I was given an opportunity to move there with several of my young engineering colleagues. This was an excellent move for the family and me.

There were no unions. Engineers could do their own experimental work, and the manager, Dr. Rudy Henning, was very strong technically.

Good Fortune 4: A new job in a wonderful community.

Six months before our move to Florida, Barbara gave birth to our second child — A brother for Skip, Glenn Edward Ely born January 20th, 1958 in Glenn Cove Long Island. We moved that summer after Glenn's birth as a family of four into a just completed three bedroom home in Clearwater.

About the time we arrived in Clearwater, one of Sperry's top sales people asked if I could meet with him and some of the lead engineers at the Naval Research Lab. I had become involved with these individuals as part of work with the navy on the early warning radar. I had flown on one of those sixteen-hour flights with the lead researcher on the navy's antisubmarine warfare program (ASW). We had become friends and Sperry was interested in the ASW program. So I ended up being the salesman's "assistant" for several months and traveled with him to the Washington labs several times. I also visited several ASW programs on the West Coast as part of this effort.

Although I enjoyed my visits to the navy labs, it was time to go back to doing actual product development. I was assigned to a couple of projects working on Sperry's Microline commercial microwave test equipment. It had been ignored for years. I got a couple of engineers involved and we made enough progress that Dr. Henning gave me responsibility for the product line and moved fifteen of us to a separate facility.

Our little group thrived. We came up with some innovative products and revitalized the whole product line. Sales grew and we even made a small profit. I personally thrived as well. Coming to work in the morning was a joy. The rest of the division paid little attention to us; the freedoms spurred us to innovation and commitment. Ultimately, we showed up at the trade show for the test equipment industry, the IEEE, in New York City. We revealed our revitalized product line and some innovative instruments. It was a big deal! We got positive coverage in the trade press and kudos from several competitors. Our success was our reward. The frustration and disappointment with most of my time at Sperry disappeared in this assignment. This opportunity defined for me what would provide fulfillment in my future career choices.

I Am READY!

All of the events and teachings that I have described in this section of the book prepared me for the challenges and excitement that lay ahead. I had learned important lessons from my parents, both from their conversations and from their behavior. My education, especially at Lehigh, had given me the fundamental science and engineering skills I needed to be successful. My summer jobs and my time with Sperry Gyroscope Company helped me understand what I did not want to do with my life and, more importantly, what I did want to do.

I was now READY for the next phase of my life.

PART II — FIRE

Shooting For Achievement

A telephone call started the process of a major career change. I began as an engineer with Hewlett Packard and made steady and surprising progress into upper management. How did this happen? What did I learn along the way? How did the atmosphere at Hewlett Packard and the founders' philosophy of management impact me and my eventual rise in the company? What was the cause of my wonderful success and good fortune that led to all I achieved? In parallel with my career, my family life was surprisingly rewarding as well. Was all this my doing or was something else guiding and supporting me along the way? These questions and the answers I discovered are the underpinnings of my life at HP–and beyond.

CHAPTER 2

Hewlett Packard, Here I Come

Leading Sperry's program for commercial microwave test equipment had me attending industry trade shows and other events where I frequently met people from Hewlett Packard. HP was the industry leader in commercial microwave test equipment. I was uniformly very impressed with the people I met who seemed knowledgeable, competent, and of high character. Then one day I got a call from Art Fong, one of the HP engineers I had met several times. He asked if I would be interested in coming out to Hewlett Packard for a job interview. WOW! You can imagine how flattered I was to be considered as a possible candidate to join this group I had so admired.

Good Fortune 5: This call opened a new opportunity.

A Big Decision

Yes, I was flattered but this opportunity was all the way across the country. My job at Sperry was the best I had so far. I led a team of fifteen engineers and because we did not need security clearances we were in a building separate from the rest of the division. It was great! No one paid any attention to us.

Barbara and I had a very nice house. By this time our second child, Glenn, was almost five and Skip was nine. We had a large group of wonderful friends. It was a good place to live and we were truly happy there. It was not clear what I should do. Should I go out to California for an interview? What if I actually got an offer?

That evening, my wife and I discussed the situation for several hours. She knew I was quite happy in my current job but also knew I did not have a very positive view of Sperry as a place to spend the rest of my career. She finally stood up and said, "Bud, you should go for the interview"(Bud was my nickname). You at least should know what they have in mind and see if the company lives up to your feelings about the people you've met."

The next day I called Art Fong and arranged to visit HP. Silicon Valley was just getting started. HP was about an $80M company in 1962. There were a few high tech companies nearby. I drove around that afternoon and was impressed. Stanford University was a few blocks away. Palo Alto was quite attractive. HP had recently moved into its first two buildings on "the hill" at 1500 Page Mill Road.

The next morning I appeared in the lobby for my "interview" which turned out to be not *an* interview but five or six interviews. Art Fong acted as my host and took me on a tour of the Microwave division lab. I was amazed! First of all, each engineer had a desk and a workbench with another engineer beside him. Their two desks were opposite the workbenches and were against the backs of the workbenches from the pair of engineers next door. No offices or walls were anywhere in sight. If you stood up you could see from one end of the lab to the other.

And there were no technicians—none. The engineers did their own experimental work, built their breadboards, and did their own testing and debugging. This was dramatically different from Sperry, Bell Labs, and other East Coast labs. This place was meant for me.

Art showed me the lab stock area. I could not believe it. It consisted of several five-foot-high bookcases, their shelves stocked with many thousands of dollars' worth of parts. It was enough to make any engineer drool. In amazement I turned to Art and asked, "How can you leave so many valuable parts in an open area where anyone can steal them?"

Art answered, "Why would anyone want to steal them? The company does not think we are thieves and you are free to take them home and use them in any personal projects. We feel that improves your skill and knowledge as an engineer."

Later, we went to an open and attractive production area. Again I noticed there were no locked stockroom cages. Now I could see possibly millions of dollars' worth of parts on rolling storage shelves close to where they were needed. I asked one of the production supervisors, "How do you control theft?" He said they have very, very little theft. "First of all, the company trusts us and we know pilfering hurts the company and would affect our profit sharing. Furthermore," he said, "our employees know if we have a bad apple that tries to pilfer something, they stop it. Finally, our employees like working here. There is no second chance. If you are dishonest and get caught, you are gone."

Interviewed The HP way

The interviewing started. It turned out to be quite intense and took several days. Three or four of the engineers or project leaders in the lab interviewed me. Bruce Wholey, the Microwave Division manager, spent quite a bit of time talking with me. And then I was taken to Barney Oliver. He was the chief technical officer for HP and head of the corporate research lab. I knew of Barney and knew he was reported to be a genius. Scared and nervous does not do justice to describe how I felt when I was led to Barney's desk and introduced. As I sat down and glanced at him, it seemed like his head was twice as big as mine (not helping my apprehension in any way). But he immediately put me at ease and showed real interest in what I had been doing. He asked questions in areas that I knew something about so I am sure those who had interviewed me earlier had briefed him. I truly enjoyed the discussion. From time to time he would ask questions beyond my knowledge; fortunately, when that happened, I simply said I did not know. I learned after I was an employee, that at least one of the interviewers was to push the interviewees beyond their knowledge to see what they did.

Before I left I met again with Bruce Wholey who told me I would be receiving a formal offer. He told the salary offer and reinforced that I could go to Stanford on the HP Honors Co-Op program to get my master's degree. In the motel, preparing to fly home the next morning, I realized this had been the most exciting few days since I had gone off to Lehigh to get an education. The decision I now faced would determine the path for the rest of my life.

That night at home in Clearwater, I told Barbara all that had happened. I'm sure she felt my enthusiasm. And when I finished and said to her, "We have a very big decision to make," she turned to me and replied, "Well, it seems as if you feel this is best for your career, and if you continue to feel that way, the kids and I will be ready to go."

So, for the next few days we considered the issues in moving from Clearwater and our wonderful group of friends. When the formal offer letter arrived from HP, I accepted the next day.

Good Fortune 6: HP – part of God's plan for me.

It is clear now that it was God's plan that I should go to Hewlett Packard. He placed me in a company environment that was highly moral and ethical; a company full of opportunity because of its consistent and long-term growth; a company staffed with competent, admirable individuals at every level. It was a very big decision for Barbara and the family to leave a location they loved with many wonderful close friends to move across the entire country from one coast to the other. It was a wonderful blessing that she did not hesitate for even a minute. Accepting HP's offer set the direction for the rest of my life.

What A Start!

My first day of employment was to be Monday, November 2, 1962. We decided I would first go alone for a few weeks to rent a house and get settled at HP. Barbara took the kids and went to New York to stay with her parents. The Cuban Missile Crisis was underway and Cuba was less than one hundred miles from Florida. Furthermore, we had to be in Pittsburg for my sister's wedding on December 29, 1962. I put Barbie and the kids on a plane for New York, hopped in the car and drove to California. I flew back to have Christmas with Barbara's parents, went to Pittsburg for the wedding and we all flew to California in early January.

We got settled in our rental home in Los Altos and Skip enrolled in third grade in the local school. Meanwhile, I was having trouble getting accepted at Stanford in the Electrical Engineering (EE) department. My undergraduate BS in Engineering Physics was nine years old and the two or three graduate courses I took at Brooklyn Poly were seven years earlier.

Stanford was concerned I could not handle the graduate level there. They finally agreed to accept me in the Industrial Engineering Department and would let me transfer to EE if I got acceptable grades in the two EE courses I intended to take that semester. It reminded me of the situation my father created for my senior year at University School. I got two As and my transfer was approved.

Good Fortune 7: Learning was essential for my career.

My initial assignment was to work on a research program using microwave wavelengths to identify gaseous compounds. It was HP policy not to use anyone hired from a competitor in any way to exploit proprietary info—not that Sperry was much of a competitor. I was partnered with a man who had a Cal PhD in Physics, and my role was to build and operate the microwave equipment to do the measurements. Since my undergraduate degree was in physics, this project was quite interesting to me.

Late one afternoon, Bill Hewlett walked in, sat down next to my desk, and started a discussion with me. He seemed very interested and knew quite a bit about what we were trying to do. He asked me about the experimental setup I had put together. We discussed that for a bit, and then launched into a discussion of the physics issues. He must have been there for a half-hour or so. Wow, after I had been at HP only a few weeks, I had an informal wide-ranging discussion with the president of the company! Nothing even close to this could have ever happened at Sperry.

Good Fortune 8: After two weeks, a chat with Bill Hewlett.

After three months, as was the practice with new engineers, they put me to work on the production floor to learn how HP products were made. Every new engineer in those days did this. The goal was to help the engineers learn what it took to get a new product into production. The production tour lasted three months and I got to know lots of people and lots of different products. I met all the supervisors and managers and about seventy others who built the products.

The three months in manufacturing taught me a lot about HP. What I had been told during my earlier interviews about the lack of pilfering was confirmed. The employees were fiercely loyal to the company. They were trusted and respected by the management and, in turn, they felt the same. There would be contests among the product lines to achieve the best quality, to reduce costs the most, or have the least days of inventory, etc. This was friendly cooperative competition; no one ever tried to win at the expense of others. Every employee wanted to help the company succeed. Employees were encouraged to come up with improvements in the way a product was made or the way it was designed, and they regularly did.

In production the workday ended at three thirty p.m. so I went back to the lab to help my partner on the research project. I'd get home about five thirty for a family dinner each night, then retire to a small niche off the living room and do my Stanford homework for a couple of hours. HP gave me time off to go to my classes during the day.

During my tour in production we found a house to buy. The problem was that our house in Clearwater had not sold so we didn't have money for a down payment. Bruce Wholey was aware of my situation and offered an HP loan for the down payment. Considering that at that point I was just an engineer who had been with the company less than six months, Barbara and I were fortunate to have found such a good company to work for. I only had to sign a simple note agreeing to pay the company the proceeds from my house when it sold.

Good Fortune 9: Yes, indeed—a company that cares.

The HP Way in Practice

After the production tour, my new lab assignment was as a project leader working on microwave swept measurement products. These were devices that could test across a range of microwave frequencies automatically. Then, six or seven months later, I was promoted to section manager for this activity. The lab had about five sections each with ten to twenty engineers.

From time to time, HP salesmen asked me to visit their customers to get direct input on what the customers wanted from HP. Before visiting the first customer, the salesman took me aside and lectured me on how HP dealt with its customers: "Make no commitments about new products until they are in production, and performance has been tested, not specs, not availability, not price or anything else." He said, "It is a sin at HP to not live up to any commitment we have made to a customer. We deal with our customers on the basis of complete honesty and trust. We don't want to do anything which weakens that trust."

When I joined the swept measurements section, there was a major project underway which included a very expensive key component made by another company. It was up to me to resolve numerous technical and pricing issues and finalize a contract to buy these components. I learned how HP dealt with suppliers during this effort. This was going to be a large deal for both HP and the supplier. I learned HP strove to be truthful, fair, and open in negotiating the contract and resolving the technical issues. This was consistent with everything else I had learned about HP. We got the deal done just in time to introduce the product on the project team's schedule.

In early 1964 we began to develop a product to fully characterize microwave devices across a range of frequencies. We called it a microwave network analyzer, a new tool for microwave engineers. This product would be a major breakthrough. To do so, we needed and used technologies from several different parts of the company. The cooperation and help from across the organization was exceptional and very typical at HP.

Finding the best and the brightest

That spring I was asked to participate in HP's college recruiting. My HP education continued. A team of three to six—depending on how many candidates were expected—from various divisions would go to the school. We each would interview a schedule of candidates and keep notes on an interview record form. At the end of the day the team would meet and discuss each candidate. We would decide if they should be invited to visit one of our labs and, if so, which one. This was a fascinating process. I quickly learned the good candidates you talked to were shared through the company, not just with the divisions interviewing them. Under the leader's direction, the team was self-disciplined in accomplishing this "sharing." Some candidates would have geographic preferences; some would obviously fit with the needs of a certain division. Deciding who should be invited for a follow-up interview and at which division could take several hours. At a school where we interviewed fifty or sixty people and decided to invite ten to fifteen, this process was not an easy one, and yet the teams worked well.

From this interviewing process I met and became friends with quite a few HP people from all over the country. I gained new insight into how HP people worked together: no maneuvering for personal advantage, no duplicity, and no hidden agendas. This matched what I had recognized in the Microwave Division and existed pretty much all over the company. Later I realized this was a key aspect of The HP Way. There was no second chance if you violated these standards of personal relationship. When you were involved in a difficult decision with other HP people, you always knew you could depend on their sincerity and truthfulness.

I came to realize what good fortune it was to have been guided to HP. I had joined a company where fairness and honesty prevailed in every relationship with fellow employees, with customers, with suppliers, and even with competitors. Backstabbing and office politics were ultimate sins and not tolerated. As a result, there was trust in the integrity and honesty of those you dealt with. All of this was a positive influence on the character of HP employees, including me. I felt it helping me become a better person. I reflected on how unfortunate that there were not more companies like this and what if society at large could operate this way.

Good Fortune 10: Character building at HP.

Amazing Career Progress

John Young became the Microwave Division manager sometime late in 1963. I had only met John a few times. After I had been section manager for about a year, John invited me to join him the next day for lunch at the nearby University Club. Wow, the University Club, this was a big deal...what could this possibly be about? That night I speculated with Barbara about the invitation. I concluded it must be he just wanted to get to know me better. But in the back of my mind was the possibility I had screwed up somehow. Had my tendency to speak out and reach decisions quickly gotten me in trouble? Clearly this was not the norm at HP.

The next day my speculation that John simply wanted to know me better seemed to be the case. He spent most of the lunch getting me to tell him about myself. But then, as we finished, he changed the topic to the current Microwave lab manager who was now my boss. John was concerned about the lab manager's performance and felt he had to replace him. He moved on to say that I was one of three men he was considering as the replacement. I was completely taken aback that I was included. I simply could not believe I was on such a list. In a couple months I would finish only my second year at HP. The other two men he was considering were about my age but had been at Hewlett Packard much longer. One of the two was another section manager in our lab. I knew him well, liked him very much and thought highly of him. I was flattered to be included with these men. They both seemed more qualified. John cautioned me our discussion was private and said he would let me know of his decision at some point after he had worked things out with the current lab manager.

When I got back from lunch I was in a daze, not quite sure what to do. I thought about the lab manager who was a very bright PhD and a few years older than me, but I could see why John might want to replace him. He was a gentleman, almost too nice, but he had trouble asserting himself. He seemed uncomfortable in his job. The lab at that point probably had about fifty engineers and he likely had been more comfortable when it was smaller.

At home that night I told Barbara, but also told her not to get her hopes up because the other two men were more qualified. So I went about my job and waited for John to send out some announcement of his choice. Nothing happened for weeks.

During this long wait, I could see the line of engineers waiting to get their semimonthly paychecks from the lab secretary. Her process was bureaucratic and made it frustrating. It occurred right in front of the lab manager. It was affecting morale. He should have done something about it. This got me thinking—what would *I* do as lab manager?

So that night I went home and worked out a one hundred-day plan if John were to select me as Microwave Lab Manager. It was just one page of handwritten bullet points for the ten items I would accomplish in the first hundred days. I called John the next day and asked if he had a little time to talk with me. When we met later that day I showed him my list of ten planned accomplishments. He asked questions about the items and I explained why I thought each was important and how I planned to accomplish it. When he finished questioning me he thanked me and said he would get back to me. The next day John announced Paul Ely was the new Microwave Lab Manager. The whole thing seemed like the impossible dream.

Good Fortune 11: Yes, an impossible dream.

Looking back now almost fifty years later this rapid progress was truly amazing. To move from engineer to project manager to section manager to lab manager over only two years in a company replete with large numbers of very competent and capable people was completely unexpected. Most had been with HP since

Graduation from college and had proven records of accomplishment. What inspired me to write up that hundred-day plan? Was John just waiting for someone to speak up? This rapid flow of promotions was more than just good fortune.

Time for action

The first hour I was in my new job I completed item one on my list. I explained to the lab secretary why she no longer had a job in the Microwave lab and took her to personnel to see if they could find something for her. There was an immediate improvement in the morale in the lab. The next morning I received a fax from an engineer who had moved from Microwave to HP in Colorado Springs. It read, "Congratulations, Paul. What was the second thing you did after you fired the lab secretary?"

My one hundred day list was finished in about sixty days. About that time I also finished my master's in electrical engineering at Stanford with grades better than my highest expectations (one B otherwise all A's). My performance at Stanford built my confidence in my new role as lab manager (some might say more confidence was not needed!).

Good Fortune 12: Grateful to have done so well at Stanford.

About six months after these events, HP sent me to a three-day course on engineering management sponsored by the American Electronics Association. The teacher went around introducing the ten or twelve people in the class. When he introduced me he said, Paul is the HP executive responsible for microwave R&D. Wow! Now at the age of thirty-three I am called an executive! I came home that night and told my wife, "Today in the class they called me an HP executive—you will have to treat me with more respect." Just how do you think that worked for me? We both had a good laugh. Isn't it funny how little things stick in your mind? I can still remember the little chill I felt when that teacher called me an executive.

Where did that little guy come from?

Not long after my promotion to Engineering manager, I was at home pondering some decision I was facing and became aware of something on my right shoulder. I turned my head and saw a miniature Jiminy Cricket standing there waving his umbrella to get my attention. He gave me some advice about the decision I was pondering and disappeared. Now, how bizarre was that! Not only bizarre, I took his advice, which worked out well. If you remember, Jiminy Cricket was Pinocchio's conscience in the Disney movie. I think I might have taken my sons to see the movie around that time, but I'm not really sure.

In any event, Jiminy started appearing to me regularly, offering advice on issues, particularly those containing moral or ethical elements. This included issues concerning The HP Way. Jiminy made sure I considered all the implications or ramifications of any such decision. My advice from Jiminy went on for several years and I came to rely on it. Clearly there was something going on here. (No, I was not going nuts!) Possibly this was simply my conscience finding a way to give me advice I might not want to hear, or possibly it was more profound than that. One thing I can say is Jiminy's advice never proved to be bad and I ended up regretting the few times I chose not to take it.

Good Fortune 13: Good advice from a trusted counselor.

This was very real at the time and remains so today. I can picture him sitting there on my shoulder. If this was just my conscience, it certainly was an unusual way to get my attention. At the time I did not question the phenomenon but I did rely on it. Where did Jiminy come from and why?

The Enjoyment of Learning and Growing

Being the Microwave Engineering manager brought me as much satisfaction and joy as any position I had before or since. The Microwave lab had so many competent and wonderful people; it made every day a delight and enabled us to develop great new products that powered the growth of the division. It was an incredible learning experience for me. Obviously, new learning in technology occurred daily, but let me cite a couple examples beyond just the technology.

Do I get a green eyeshade?

When I became Engineering manager, the budget for the year ahead was already set. But I started carefully studying the monthly expense reports so I would be ready for the 1965 budget. The report was almost incomprehensible and the accountant assigned to work with me could not explain it. One day another person filled in and he was different. In a few hours working together we discovered several problems with the report and opportunities to better manage expenses. I went to John Young and asked to have this guy assigned to work with me. John agreed and that accountant, John Russell, was with me constantly throughout my career at HP and beyond. He became a valued friend and a big contributor to my success.

Good Fortune 14: John's help and friendship, a true blessing.

How do we get more money?

Now I had a teacher and gained enough knowledge in accounting to be dangerous. As we prepared the next year's budget, the amount we had been told we could spend did not provide enough to hire as many engineers as needed to staff the exciting products we were ready to start. So I went to John Young to ask for more money. I took my desired project list into John and explained how great each project was. John listened patiently to my pitch and said he was truly impressed and then explained very succinctly how I could get more money. He said, "Paul, with very few exceptions, HP Divisions may spend eight percent of their prior year's sales for R&D. If you want to have more money next year, be sure you use this year's money to get out new products that create on-going growth. Also, keep in mind, if you don't invest enough in existing products to keep them viable, their decline will offset the growth from new products."

I was disappointed that he would not just hand out some more bucks but I also realized how much freedom this approach provided. Wow, what a motivator and wonderful way to manage for profitable growth. This was a "market approach" to allocating investments. No centralized planning person was allocating those investments. This magically simple approach provided funds for those labs that created growth and reduced it for the less successful.

Good Fortune 15: A unique way to earn my own budget.

How did we do?

I was the Engineering manager for four or so years and it was exciting. We got out lots of new products, which helped the division grow significantly. We not only introduced important new products, we also developed important new technologies. We developed a process to build miniature microwave circuits on sapphire chips with metal thin films as waveguides (waveguides were normally rectangular metallic pipes that contain and guide the microwave signals). These microcircuits greatly reduced the size, weight, and cost of microwave components and improved their performance. These were essential building blocks for many of our new instruments.

Another major development was the capability to design and manufacture transistors, which could operate at microwave frequency. These gave us important competitive advantages. The devices we could buy were very limited in power and frequency range. Both of these technologies required very expensive manufacturing facilities with clean rooms and processing equipment, much like those used in the semiconductor industry.

The lessons keep coming

I really enjoyed and learned much while working for John Young. I could go to him with one of my initiatives, and he would start asking me questions and would point out possible problems. He never actually told me not to do something but I quickly learned how to discern the ideas he did not like, and sometimes would just drop them, but more often took his concerns very seriously and came up with adjustments to avoid the pitfalls. He told me once, "Paul, no wonder you so often succeed. You adjust the goals as you go along!" Is there a lesson here?

My father had taught me that conventional wisdom was frequently not right. One such example was that, while most companies doing complex technical work try to hire people with considerable related experience (conventional wisdom), HP concentrated on hiring people right out of school. Early on I asked about this and was told that people with prior experience tend to go back and do it the same way over again, but those starting fresh are much more likely to find an innovative approach. So, throughout my career, when conventional wisdom was explicitly or implicitly the reason for doing or not doing something, I found opportunity lurking. This is a much more general principle than the simple example above and is akin to what's called "thinking outside the box." It applies to every kind of situation: human resources, products and product features, in-house processes and so on. Things change! Frequently, there are unseen or unconsidered factors. This principle played a much bigger role in my career and life than is obvious from this paragraph. I made a practice of defying the conventional wisdom.

Good Fortune 16: A principle repeatedly valuable.

Knowledge from blots

HP agreed to participate in a study concerning the effect of rapid change on society. The Microwave lab was chosen as the HP organization to be involved. The researcher, Michael Maccoby, was a disciple of Erick Fromm at Harvard. Maccoby wrote a book titled *The Gamesman*, summarizing what he found in hundreds of in-depth interviews of people at IBM and HP. The Rorschach Inkblot test was one of his tools to learn about people. I wasn't concerned about taking the test, and, although I was usually quite effective in revealing no more than I chose to on such tests, I decided not to attempt to control the outcome this time. It was just a few inkblots—no problem! After all, who could learn anything about me from a few stupid inkblots? So I reacted openly and honestly to what I saw in the ten inkblots. The test took less than ten minutes. At the end he asked if I would like to know what he had learned. I said yes, of course, barely suppressing a condescending giggle.

He then rattled off three or so things that I had never recognized about myself but immediately realized were true. Several were not particularly positive but all added importantly to my self-understanding. And then he said something had happened he had never experienced in any of the thousand or more inkblot tests he had administered. He said, "You saw movement in every one of the inkblots. Paul, you see everything in life as in motion; you see nothing as standing still." We talked about this for some time as he tried to help me interpret this. In any case, I told him how amazed I was that he could learn so much in such a short time from ten apparently random inkblot images. I thanked him profusely for what I had learned about myself and left, still confused over the implications of that last finding.

As time passed I was conscious of this characteristic and concluded that it was somehow related to my enjoyment of working in an industry experiencing rapid change.

Good Fortune 17: Ink blots added to my self-knowledge.

What a wonderful school

My six years at HP had been a constant learning experience: my master's degree at Stanford; my envelopment in The HP Way and its effect on my character; the advanced technologies I was working with; and the improvement in my management skills. As an engineering manager, I learned constantly from my peers. All the lab managers would find every excuse to get together at trade shows, company meetings, or just visiting one another. We would discuss our problems and new organizational ideas we had been testing, in addition to product plans and tech issues. Furthermore, in my frequent interactions with other engineering managers, we often discussed what we valued in the men we reported to.

I was fortunate to have a close relationship with John Young, a very effective general manager, and I had opportunities for direct interaction with other general managers. It was a terrific training ground to see the decisions being made and then what the results were. I also had opportunities to interact directly with Bill and Dave.

Good Fortune 18: Continuous learning of enormous value.

One particular meeting with Dave Packard has remained one of my favorites. The company had just completed the development of its first minicomputer. As the first few pilot production units were nearing completion, Dave notified all the engineering managers that the very first unit would go to the lab that had the best proposal for its use in an instrument system. He invited all the lab managers to tell him why they should get the first computer. A key section manager and I already had a system concept that we could hardly wait to implement. It was for an automatic network analyzer that would use HP's first minicomputer to greatly increase the accuracy and speed of characterizing microwave devices with the new network analyzer mentioned earlier.

We immediately started writing up a comprehensive proposal explaining the system we wanted to build and why the project would make an important contribution. The next morning we called Dave and made an appointment to see him that afternoon to present our proposal. The two of us started to present our hand-written plan but Dave soon stopped us and said, "Okay, Paul, you two can have the first 2116 computer."

We were delighted, of course, but also amazed. I said, "Dave, we spent a lot of time preparing a presentation that we thought was very powerful. Why did you give us the computer before we barely got started?"

Dave responded, "You two are so completely committed to this project, I am confident one way or the other much good will come out of it." Dave was simply evaluating our commitment while we were trying to persuade him with technical details. What is the lesson here?

Good Fortune 19: Commitment created opportunity.

Once More a Big Step Forward

In 1968 John Young was promoted to Vice President and became the first head of the Electronics Products Group that included the Microwave Division along with all the other instrument divisions. John selected me to be his replacement as Microwave Division Manager. Here I was, thirty-six years old, only six years with Hewlett Packard and now the general manager of one of the company's larger divisions. I felt highly honored and incredibly blessed.

Good Fortune 20: A very big opportunity.

Here was one more wonderful promotion. Four successful years as the Division Engineering Manager certainly helped. But what created that success? It would be comforting to credit it to my great skill and talent, but looking back, now I see something else was going on. The Microwave lab was blessed with a team of talented individuals. It seemed at just the right time with just the right skills some individual would blossom forth. An individual would unexpectedly sprout a valuable new concept. Another would solve a sticky problem seemingly beyond his capabilities. This happened over and over again. Yes, we had a very good team, but this is not just an effort to give credit to the team. It was almost magical! This sort of thing continued throughout much of my HP career. Just the right people always seemed to be there to help just when they were needed.

Good Fortune 21: The right people at the right time.

Just before my promotion, my secretary for the prior several years announced she was getting married and would be leaving.

She said not to worry; she would help me find a replacement. She was an excellent secretary, efficient, very competent, pleasant and helpful to all. She claimed she knew the person she felt would be perfect for me and asked me to interview Geri Cherem. At that point Geri worked in the lab as the supervisor of about seven women doing printed circuit layout. When I interviewed Geri it became apparent she had not been looking for a new job but had commented to my current secretary how unpleasant it was supervising a group of women. Geri had all the qualifications, fast typing, took dictation, and had a great personality. All the lab engineers knew her and she was well-liked. So I gave her an offer and she accepted. That turned out to be a very good decision.

She was a humble, gentle, soft-spoken person who was very easy to talk with. It turned out she was also very competent, a wonderful organizer, always on top of everything I asked of her. People would come to her when they wanted me to know something but were afraid to say it to me directly. She knew how intense I was and was able to calm me down and helped me to slow down so I could think things through carefully. She was my secretary for my entire career at HP and for many years afterward.

Good Fortune 22: Geri, destined for a major role in my life.

Little things mean a lot!

This promotion had come unexpectedly and the division was running well. It occurred to me that it was better to be promoted to head an organization that needed fixing than one that was running well where there was the possibility I could screw it up.

To start, as division manager I decided to move my desk to the middle of the production floor. I did two things to help make the manufacturing employees feel more comfortable talking to me. In those days HP had coffee breaks for all employees and people would congregate and chat at the coffee stations. So each day I would stroll over to a different coffee station and start a conversation. In addition, we set up weekly lunch "communication meetings" for about twenty regular production employees. We met for thirty minutes while everyone ate. It took a little time to get people talking but by the end of the meeting, usually there would have been a lively discussion.

At one of these lunch meetings, an employee who had been very quiet asked if she could tell me about the Coke machine. I learned that a line would build up at the one vending machine which, for many, could use up the half-hour lunch period. Although it took some time and persuading on my part we got four new machines from the vendor. Wow, that was really appreciated and helped build a relationship with the production team

I spent about a year with my desk on the production floor and learned much about HP and its people from that experience. It is amazing how taking the time to resolve little things can provide big benefits.

Once again to Stanford

A few months after I was promoted to General Manager, Hewlett Packard sent me to an eight-week executive MBA program at Stanford. This was an incredible learning experience of many dimensions. Of course one of those dimensions was the course content and teaching. We were assigned to read dozens of books during those eight weeks. We went to class all day except for a short time in the late afternoon when we could read or get some exercise playing volleyball, etc. In the evenings we had seminars or met in small groups to play roles in case study problems. We had weekends off, but in general, spent most of the time reading.

Although my home was ten minutes from the Stanford campus, I lived in the dorm with the rest of the class during the week and went home Saturday and Sunday. There were one hundred and twenty people in the class. About sixty were International, mostly the UK and its former colonies, and a few French and Italians. I was thirty-seven. There were very few others under forty, and the younger group tended to hang out together.

Another dimension beyond just the course content was getting to know so many people from all over the world. Several became life-long friends. The evening case study problem solving was particularly valuable in getting to know how the older, more experienced men approached the problems. Most were high-level executives from large well-known East Coast and European companies. They seemed constrained to the conventional wisdom, whereas the few mostly younger men from the West Coast, Australia, and South Africa came up with more unique and innovative solutions to the case problems. When I put forth an approach to an issue built on The HP Way, it was often considered impractical and idealistic.

Risky business

This experience gave me confidence in HP and in myself...that is, until I learned the results of a risk aversion test the class took toward the end of the eight-week term. My test score indicated I was the second most risk-averse person in the class of one hundred and twenty. How could this be! Most of these people were overly cautious and had not had an innovative thought in recent memory. I was devastated, and my confidence badly bruised. After a day or two I went to see the professor who had given the test. He may have been expecting me as he had my test handy. We went over it together and he pointed out where my answers had shown me to be risk-averse.

He gave me a clean copy of the test to study in my room. As I did that, my confidence slowly returned. My HP training had not let me down and fully explained my score. Of the test questions, when there was a possibility of a big loss, I avoided that investment. As Engineering Manager I had a list of as many as one hundred product investments we could choose but could only afford ten or, at most, fifteen. We always had many with the potential for great future returns but very little possibility of a major downside. Of course, on the list there were some that had very big potential but had very big downsides, usually also requiring lots of time and lots of money before there were any results. Some were risky because a major technical breakthrough was required.

Often we reduced the risk by exploring the technology with a small effort before we staffed up a major project. I had always allocated fifteen percent of the budget to such investigations. Structuring our efforts to avoid the need for major front-end investments until we minimized the uncertainty was an HP tenet. Packard used to say "an elephant is eaten a bite at a time." In a similar vein, when Packard went to the government to serve as Deputy Secretary of Defense, he established a "Fly Before Buy" policy.

My eight weeks at Stanford that summer were a blessing. It brought me much knowledge that was important to my future roles in management. It confirmed how fortunate I was to be an HP employee and further built my faith in The HP Way.

Good Fortune 23: Eight weeks at Stanford–a blessing.

It's All About People!

On my return to work after my eight weeks at Stanford, there were signs the person I had selected to be the manufacturing manager was having a difficult time in his job. He had been in his job for about six months at that point. So I set out to help him be successful. He had a polished resume—undergraduate engineering degree, a couple years as a naval officer, then a Harvard MBA and a good bit of HP manufacturing experience. However, he had difficulty putting his thoughts into action and then getting his team to go forward with them. He was unassertive and often communicated uncertainty about what should be done. For six more months, which were very painful for both of us, I tried everything I could think of to help him succeed. I finally recognized that he was just not suited for this kind of line responsibility and nothing I could do would change that. It should not have taken me so long to recognize this.

There were also lessons to be learned from the man who replaced him. Mac, the replacement, was easy to underestimate and had nothing comparable to the pedigree of my original choice. He had an engineering degree from a Cal State college. He had worked in the lab for a few years and then had become a section manager in Production. None would call him brilliant, but he had a good mind and far more than his share of common sense. His easygoing manner belied a strong results-oriented drive. His small ego allowed him to accept good ideas from anyone on his team.

Soon Mac had the organization humming, and before long began to be recognized as one of HP's best manufacturing managers. He and his team made it possible to make important reductions in the time it took to get new products reliably into production and worked closely with the lab engineers to reduce production costs. No one underestimated him now.

Good Fortune 24: The right people at the right time.

This experience was both a lesson and good fortune. The lesson was that it's not good credentials that determine success, it's the person—his capabilities and character. It was good fortune because, again, just when needed, up sprouted the man to do the job. Mac was a very valuable addition to the Division management team.

Time to move again

It was time to move my desk again. My replacement as Engineering Manager was doing an excellent job and the last thing he needed was to have the former manager sitting around looking over his shoulder. So I moved my desk to the marketing area, taking care to be in a secluded location in a corner far from where the marketing manager sat.

Division marketing at HP had basically two functions: product marketing and sales support for the sales force. All the divisions were essentially trying to earn as much time as possible from the sales people. Good products that customers want was the most important way get attention from the sales team, but sales training and superior support still played a major role.

We had a retired marine as Sales Support Manager who had told his team he did not want any phone in the department to ring more than twice before it was answered. He made clear he meant it by going into drill sergeant mode when a senior staffer did not think it meant him.

The Marketing Department was led by a strong manager who was doing a good job (took me two tries to get the right one). The division continued its steady flow of new products, producing good growth. The investments in microwave integrated circuits and microwave transistors now were giving our latest products real competitive advantages in both performance and price. There was now a team of very competent managers leading the division with many very capable people at the next level.

Good Fortune 25: Blessed with exceptional talent.

Caring for employees

The economy was about to suffer a recession, particularly in military spending. Dave Packard had taken a leave from HP to become Deputy Secretary of Defense. He had been charged with achieving major reductions in defense expenditures as the Nixon administration was trying to wind down the war in Vietnam. He succeeded. HP, along with much of the nation, felt the result. The entire company was hard hit by the economic situation. We were building products faster than the orders were coming in. Something had to be done. Hewlett Packard had never had a layoff and never wanted to. The company had historically turned down large government contract opportunities just to avoid the "boom and bust" difficulties of many government contractors.

It was up to Bill Hewlett to find a solution. He came up with an approach that the employees felt was fair and appropriate. The entire work force from Bill on down would share in the solution. We called it the "9 Day Fortnight." *Everyone* would take one day off without pay every two weeks. The production people got a three-day weekend but most of the engineers and supervisors voluntarily worked all ten days.

This kind of an approach was typical of HP. We had one of the most generous health insurance programs. It included catastrophic insurance to provide two-thirds of full-time salary for up to a year for those with medical problems that kept them from work. HP was one of the first U.S. companies to adopt flextime and paid time off (PTO). PTO combined sick leave and vacation, so unused sick leave was available for vacation. In general, HP was as innovative with its benefit policies as it was with its products. Another example was a stock purchase plan that allowed all employees to purchase at eighty-five percent of the lowest market price at the beginning or end of each six-month period. There was a very broad stock option program (I received a 300-share option about a year after I joined the company). After ten years of employment, <u>every</u> employee received ten shares of HP stock. Thousands of HP employees became wealthy by buying and holding HP stock—HP stock averaged twenty percent growth per year for many decades.

HP had a profit-sharing plan that paid anywhere from two percent to six percent of your annual income based on the company's performance that year. Everybody received the same percent of their salary. The company also set aside twelve and one-half percent of profit for a retirement program. Each employee was credited with the same percent of his or her salary and then vested at ten percent for each year of employment. If you left the company, the vested amount went with you

HP's education benefits were also very favorable. Any technical or professional employee could attend local colleges to get advanced degrees or even a bachelor's degree at company expense. I got my master's degree in Electrical Engineering at Stanford on the Honors Co-op program, which HP had helped originate. Students in this program got time off to attend the regular class schedule at Stanford. Several test technicians went all the way through to get a bachelor's degree, followed by an advanced degree.

Good Fortune 26: Exceptional care for employees.

Laughter is the Best Policy!

Humor was an important aspect of life at HP. It was encouraged. Anybody was fair game. Kidding others about their personality traits and foibles in a fun and respectful way was used to reduce tension and to help people, including managers, be aware of their foibles. I certainly was endowed with abundant material for this teasing.

As an engineer with the company for only a few weeks, I had to contact a supplier across country and asked the company operator to place the call. She hesitated at first and then asked if she might give me a suggestion that could save the company some money. "Of course," I said. She then quipped, "Mr. Ely, if you just use the stairs and go up to the roof, I am quite sure they can hear you in New York!" That was certainly better and more effective than saying, "Mr. Ely, you are so loud you are hurting my ears."

It appeared that others thought my voice was loud and distracting. After I moved my desk to the Marketing Department. I had been traveling to Europe to visit customers and when I returned to the marketing area, I found my desk enclosed in a cubicle with glass extensions going all the way to the ceiling. I was told it was not an office (no one at HP had offices except Bill and Dave) but it was a "cone of silence." A TV show at that time called "Get Smart" featured Maxwell Smart who used a "cone of silence" to convey secrecy. I used that "cone of silence" as my office for several years and peace reigned in the Microwave Marketing Department.

Two or three years after I became Division Manager, Microwave became the largest division in the company. We finally had passed the division managed by my colleague Al Bagley. In those days the divisions had "beer busts" anytime there was something to celebrate. A beer bust was a party at the end of the workday for all the employees, offering barbequed hot dogs and hamburgers with fixings, and beer. Our division had a wonderful, big patio surrounded by buildings. To celebrate our new number one status, a large structure two stories high in the form of the number one had been built mostly of cardboard and pallet wood. The base formed an elevated stage which I was to mount and congratulate everyone.

There were hundreds of people in the patio when I climbed the eight or so feet to the stage. As I started to speak a trapdoor directly above in the overhang of the number one opened and a huge amount of water rained down on my head, followed by a sea of water balloons. Everyone loved it! I was soaked from head to toe. I should have known some such thing would have been planned. We had invited Al Bagley and his division to come and join us to celebrate their displacement, and they particularly enjoyed my being doused. Of course no one would ever admit to having organized this dastardly deed, but it certainly made for a good party.

HP humor kept you in your place

The year following the economic problem, in preparation for the division annual management meeting, I convinced Bill Hewlett to do a video interview to get his recommendations for the division goals for the year ahead. I should have known better because Al Bagley got a hold of one of Bill's comments. Bill had suggested that Microwave should "regain the initiative in its new product program" which had been a little less dramatic in the down economy. Well we had invited Al and his division to come up to another of those beer busts celebrating our plans for the coming year. All and his team joined us and brought with them hundreds of flaming pink stickers that said:

HMRI
Help Microwave Regain the Initiative

Before we realized what was going on they had placed these everywhere, on people's desks, on the windows, on managers' cars. It took me a week or more to get this off the front of my car hood without removing the paint. And of course for many weeks afterward they would greet us with "HMRI" any time they saw one of us.

Each year HP had an offsite management meeting. During my last year or two as an engineering manager, I had been invited. At that point there would only be fifty or sixty attending so it was a big deal to go. The agenda would include an evaluation of the past year's performance, usually by Bill or Dave; expectations for the current year; presentations on new corporate initiatives; breakout sessions on timely topics; and talks by invited outside experts.

Before dinner on the first night everyone was invited into the dining room a few minutes early. All around the walls were pictures of various company managers with humorous thought or talk balloons. I was an easy target. There would be twenty or so of these around the dining room walls getting in digs for many attendees. After dinner there was a skit with the top company executives as the actors. They would be given a script as they came on stage that would portray managers, humorously depicting their idiosyncrasies or characteristics. One of these skits was the source of the Ready, Fire, Aim slogan applied to me by my coworkers. By the end of the evening everyone would be aching from laughing so hard.

Not so funny

But I remember one such meeting where most everyone thought he had done a good job that year. After most of the presentations on the prior year's results, Dave got up to speak and made it clear immediately that he was not happy with our performance. He was particularly peeved at the continued increases in the divisional administrative costs and inventory. He presented a list of all the divisions ranked in order of performance in each category.

You did not want to be at the bottom of either list. He made a statement such as "If you can't get your house in order" he would get someone who could. From then on, each year when the meeting started, there would be a chart(s) ranking the measure(s) that were the focus that year. There would be a line across the list at the corporate average. Below that line was a risky place to be. The prior year's chart would also be posted with the current year's rankings. These simple ranking charts kept the entire company striving for continuous improvement. The division at the top worked to stay there and the ones below average at the least wanted to show improvement. If you want to improve something, measure it and either compare to a high standard or to the achievements of others.

Lessons from the HP University

HP, for me, was a university of management. Best of all, we had Bill and Dave demonstrating by their actions how to let go to provide their managers the freedom to innovate and perform. They also demonstrated how to take charge when things were not going well and set in motion necessary change. They set the model for integrity. They were often thought of as paternalistic but, if so, they set very high standards and expectations, and when these were not met, the responsible managers were replaced. When that happened, those managers were treated with dignity and provided a second chance in a different kind of assignment.

Packard was quoted as saying, "You can't manage without knowing the territory."

In learning my territory, my prime method was to "wander around," and during my five years as General Manager I took advantage of my location in Manufacturing and Marketing to wander every day asking questions or even just chatting with people. This was the corollary to the "open door" policy. Not only could you freely approach higher-ups, but also you could expect to have those same higher-ups wandering through the groups you managed. Nothing was hidden. HP managers quickly learned to face up to issues as soon as they arose. The whole process encouraged honesty and forthrightness. Keeping a problem hidden did not work.

The decentralized organization that Bill and Dave built provided important benefits. It spread responsibility broadly throughout the company, unleashing opportunities for innovation and initiative to large numbers of people. It encouraged managers at every level to do the same for those they managed.

Many lessons have been highlighted throughout this chapter. One of the lessons I learned over and over was to always question the conventional wisdom and the status quo. I learned that you can "have your cake and eat it too," that "the glass is almost always half full," that when I was told, "Paul, you can't do that" or "We tried that, it won't work," there was probably opportunity lurking there someplace.

I learned much from John Young. He was a good coach, giving me plenty of freedom but was always there when I wanted his advice. The example he provided as general manager served to prepare me for my promotion to that role. I was very fortunate to report to him throughout my entire career with only a couple of short gaps. His guidance was a major influence on my success.

I also learned an enormous amount from my peers. As an engineering manager I benefited by having five or more bright, capable people in similar jobs in other divisions. We met often and freely shared ideas and concepts in HP's environment of trust and shared goals. And this process was repeated with other general managers when I became one. Sharing and openness provided many examples of what worked and, occasionally, what did not work. I was blessed at HP with many people to emulate. What a learning experience!

Good Fortune 27: More sources of learning.

First and foremost, among the many lessons were those that had grown my understanding and deep commitment to The HP Way. To HP employees, The HP Way was a total culture that guided every aspect of life at HP. On the next page is my view of what made this company so unique.

.

The HP Way

Integrity was expected in everything, fairness and honesty in all relationships; fellow employees, customers, suppliers, competitors, etc. Principle overcame pragmatism. Backstabbing and office politics were ultimate sins. As a corollary, there was trust in the integrity and honesty of those you dealt with. Because of this, HP was a positive influence on the character of its employees; they felt good when they went home at night. I certainly believe HP had a very positive influence on my character.

Leadership was the goal in everything the company did; products, employee and customer relations, community involvement, etc. Bold initiatives were encouraged, provided you could "bootstrap" your way to success (i.e., Dave's "fly before buy" policy at the Pentagon). To managers, leadership meant best inventory turns, best quality record, best new product program, etc. "Average" was a dirty word. Bill and Dave provided leadership by example. As the company grew, they understood the few decisions that required their attention but trusted the organization to handle everything else. They did not wait for consensus: if desirable, they created it; if not, they went forward.

Opportunism was HP's guiding growth strategy. This took place within a loose framework, partly financial, partly organizational, but there was no grand plan for the company's evolution. The decentralized organization promoted opportunism. Bill Hewlett often declined to "rationalize" overlapping programs with only the admonition that it would be foolish to continue a project that was second best. In this light, consider the path by which HP attained leadership in printers.

HP People made it all happen. HP's recruiting program was extraordinary; hiring not only the best and brightest, but those with initiative and enthusiasm as well. High standards of performance were combined with great patience in helping individuals succeed. Individuals were provided with freedom and opportunity to grow. The company was an early innovator in employee education and training.

Good Fortune 28: The "HP WAY"

63

After almost ten years, my days in the Microwave Division were about to end. I had come to know and highly value the trust and respect for others, so fundamental to The HP Way. I had learned what integrity really meant because I had seen it in practice by many throughout the company. I understood this experience had improved my character. It changed my entire understanding of how organizations can and should operate. It made every day joyful and made me proud of the organization of which I was a part.

Good Fortune 29: Ten years of comprehensive training.

*Yes — **what a fantastic learning experience**. I do believe God guided me to this company to gain this learning. The learning contributed to my ongoing career but was necessary preparation for the Lord's intent to use me somehow for His work in the future.*

CHAPTER 3

An Exciting New Challenge

Packard arrived back from his tour in the Pentagon in late 1972, just as HP was about to launch a bond offering to provide cash for the business. This was a big step for the company and a major departure from the company's long-standing policy against borrowing. Dave asked Bill to hold back the bond offering for a week or so to see if he could come up with a way to avoid taking on this debt. It did not take him long. Dave studied several operations and concluded the company could do a better job of managing its assets. He toured many of HP's major facilities to assure himself this could be done and to make clear to the managers what they needed to accomplish. Sure enough! Improvements came quickly and within a few years HP became a leader in asset management.

Problems in HP's Computer Business

Once the solutions were underway to resolve the debt offering, Dave turned his attention to issues in HP's Computer Division. He toured the division in Cupertino and found the company had been selling a new type of computer before it had been fully developed. This was a no-no for HP and was particularly upsetting to Dave.

The company had a long-standing policy that products were not to be sold or even marketed until development was complete and a production pilot run had been completed and tested. Unfortunately, the marketing and sales groups had been very successful in selling a product that did not exist. Approximately fifty units had been sold, costing several hundred thousand dollars, each on the basis of target specs created by marketing. Engineering was having problems achieving anything close to marketing's specs. The press was now writing articles about the situation. This kind of situation damaged HP's reputation for integrity and was what HP strove to avoid by its long-standing policies. Dave was understandably very upset and was further embarrassed as the author of the "fly-before-buy policy" he had instituted at the Pentagon.

While sitting at my desk one afternoon in February 1973, Dave called and asked if I could come over to his office. I got there in about three minutes (feet barely touching the floor) and found him waiting for me. After I was seated he asked if I knew about the problems in Cupertino (the location of the Computer Division, about twenty minutes away). I said I did, in general. He gave me a quick overview of the situation as he saw it. He then said he would like me to go there as Division Manager to "straighten out the situation." He made clear that part of this assignment was to help the division understand "how we do things at Hewlett Packard." He said I could take overnight to make sure I wanted to do this and to come the next morning and tell him and Bill of my decision.

Good Fortune 30: Huge opportunity but a big challenge.

Magical autopilot

Of course there was not much of a decision for me to make that evening. I knew this would have been discussed with my boss, John Young, and he must have felt I could do what was required. So far my career at HP seemed like it was guided by a magical autopilot. I was just following my nose, concentrating on doing a good job, and seeming to glide through the chairs smoothly and quickly—engineer, project leader, section manager, lab manager, division manager. Something new unfolded every few years to challenge me and move me forward.

Nonetheless, my magical autopilot was now heading in a completely new direction. The Computer Division was a different and far more competitive business where HP was not a leader. The technology was different, the markets were different and the people were different. You'd think my Jiminy Cricket would have been shouting in my ear and beating me with his cane saying, "Don't do this!" But somehow, there was no doubt in my mind, just this unexplained confidence, that had taken hold and progressed with each step I had taken so far in my HP career.

So the next morning about eight thirty I went to see Bill and Dave and told them I would go to Cupertino and was excited by the challenge. We talked for a bit and then I asked how soon they wanted me to start in Cupertino. Dave responded, "Would noon be too soon?" So by noon I moved to Cupertino with my secretary Geri, and our desks.

Magical help for me

I started by walking around and talking to people to develop an understanding of how they got into this mess and what I might do to resolve the issues. I knew a few of them. After a day or so I realized something strange was going on in the conversations I was having with people. An individual would say a couple sentences, but I seemed to have received several paragraphs of valuable information. This was more than just reading between the lines.

The effect of all this extra information was to build my understanding of the situation, the people and their capabilities, at an amazing pace. This blizzard of information continued for four or five weeks and then my conversations slowly returned to normal. Later in my career I had another similar experience of this "extrasensory perception" when I came to "hear" much more than the words actually spoken.

Good Fortune 31: Supernatural help!

This "between the lines" information was not my imagination. As I followed up on what I "heard" it quickly became clear it was extremely useful in helping me sort out the situation and provided valuable insight into individual agendas. These experiences likely saved lots of time and saved me from making important mistakes.

It was obvious that there was very little communication going on between the marketing and engineering teams and what was taking place was not necessarily positive. Even worse, the marketing group was set to move to a separate facility across the street, further attenuating communication. I made clear the move was not going to happen.

It was also painfully obvious that we were spending much more on marketing than we could afford. We had quite a few top notch marketing people and many of them saw the handwriting on the wall and left of their own volition. Later, when I recruited the former Microwave Finance Manager to come and help me, I discovered we had been spending almost twice as much in marketing as in engineering. This might be okay if we were just putting flowers on toilet paper to sell but we were developing technologically advanced computers intended to transform an important segment of the computer industry.

Facing the facts

Evaluating the issues affecting the new business computer revealed that we were not going to achieve in the foreseeable future anything close to the specs our customers had been sold. With the help of a key marketing manager, we personally visited each and every customer to apologize, to make clear what our status really was and offer some alternatives. We told them of course they could cancel their order at any time, or they could maintain their order but it would be several months before even the limited capability machine could be delivered. Finally, we offered to loan them one of our existing timesharing machines, which could support lots of terminals but not in business transaction-processing applications.

I did not look forward to those visits but it turned out not to be as bad as I expected. No one threw things at me or threatened to sue. Less than half of the orders were canceled. The company got compliments for being so forthright and for the sincere apologies. Actually, it turned out to be a positive experience.

Good Fortune 32: The HP Way with customers succeeded.

The customer meetings took almost a month. Between those trips much of my time was spent with the engineering team working on the new business computer causing all the issues. This computer, the HP 3000, had a very unique architecture and was a machine intended for business transaction processing. The engineers went to work to complete the development of a product with specs they felt were achievable. It took a couple months to begin shipping a limited performance version and a couple years to turn it into a product HP could be proud of.

The task of creating market success for the HP 3000 will be discussed later in this book.

Meanwhile, there were plenty of other problems that needed attention. HP's original minicomputer line, the HP2100, was used in technical applications, such as measurement data collection, and machine control. The current model had been introduced in 1970 and by 1973 was badly in need of an upgrade. This product line had been the basis for all of the company's computer revenues. There was a new model under development called the 21MX. The development team was in a quandary over what memory system to use. They could continue with core memory that was costly and had limited performance.

Core memory had been used throughout the computer industry in the early years, but Texas Instruments and one or two others claimed semiconductor memory chips would soon be in production. After they briefed me on their dilemma, I said, "Let's go for it and be the first company to use semiconductor memory."

Encouraging the Division to take reasonable risks to get a step ahead of the competition became my role for a few years. Things moved fast in the computer business and HP was far from in a leading position. We were not going to become a leader by simply following the prevailing wisdom.

That became my pattern for the next several years. "Good fortune" was with me. Most of the risky decisions I made came out favorably. As the years went by, the growing Cupertino team learned that at Hewlett Packard, if you fell short of an ambitious goal you were not punished; you got another chance.

Good Fortune 33: Seeking leadership leads to success.

Yes, opportunity seemed to be lurking every time someone told me "we tried that," "it won't work," "it's too big," "it's too small," and "everyone knows that's impossible." My early experience on HP recruiting teams showed me that the bright young engineers we hired right out of school often came up with far more innovative solutions than seasoned experts. Our young, inexperienced engineers might take a little longer but frequently came up with beautifully simple solutions. Barney Oliver would often say "complex is ugly, simple is beautiful, and simplicity often provides the best solution." But I diverge somewhat.

Wandering into problems

Both Bill and Dave used management by wandering around. As you may recall, that's how I first met Bill—when he wandered into the lab and stopped to talk with me. I was wandering around one day when I stated talking to one of the techs working in the system integration area and found out when they received all the pieces of a system, the computer, interface cards, cables and various peripherals, it took more than a week to get them working together. He also told me that the field installation people who assembled that same system later for the customer were also grumbling because it still took them a long time to get the system up and running.

When I got back to my desk I called the group that did the field installation to get their side of the story. I found it took them another week to get the items working together. They did not feel the in-house group could possibly be doing a good job. My first reaction was we are not gaining anything by putting it together in the factory; let's just ship to the customer directly and have our people do it there. The storm of protest was enormous. "Paul, you're crazy, IBM does it like we do, so does DEC and all the other computer companies. The customers won't like it and it will be

71

embarrassing to the company." (Sounds like the conventional wisdom again. There must be an opportunity here someplace.)

When this issue came up, it was late spring. I had been there for a few months. "I hear you," I said, and added, "You have all summer to solve all the issues, but on September 30 we start shipping direct and do no integration in the factory."

With audible grumbling, they agreed to this and both teams worked together to identify what was going on and how to solve it. Guess what? We did start shipping direct in September and it went pretty well. Initially, without any factory integration, the onsite integration remained about the same, but after a couple more months, the systems were up and running in a couple days. Customers were happy, the field team was happy, we saved a bunch of money, and both groups were proud of what they had accomplished.

Good Fortune 34: The team made it work.

New Location, New Products

The Cupertino Division growth was becoming unwieldy with two computer families: the HP2100 series and the HP3000, along with various peripherals and software. Peripherals are used with computers to make a computer system; for example, printers, storage devices, terminals, and so forth. Most of the peripherals were purchased but still required engineering evaluation teams and incoming tests. We did make a few of the peripherals but needed to make more in-house. Printers and data storage disks were particular problems and had generally been developed by our suppliers for the mainframe business. The company had identified Boise as a promising location for an HP plant. I visited

Boise and liked what I saw and decided to go ahead and start an organization there to develop and produce printers in-house.

HP had acquired a company that made magnetic tape data storage drives a few years earlier, which was part of the Computer Division but located in a separate facility. It had been decided this operation could be moved to Boise to start a division there. The product line was not strategic for HP's computer family and would be discontinued in a few years. Our goal was to have designed a printer suitable for HP systems and to have it in production before it was time to discontinue the tape product. Ray Smelek was the general manager of the tape drive organization and had been selected by the prior management team to go to Boise. I knew Ray from his early days in the Microwave Division and concurred with the decision. He rented a temporary facility to use for the startup and selected a few key people to transfer to Boise. We started manufacturing the tape drives there before the end of the year. I helped Ray negotiate a deal to get the rights to an interesting dot matrix impact line printer technology. In a couple of years we had developed our own version of the technology and were shipping units. The dot matrix approach was not widely accepted at the time but quickly became the focus of the HP printer program.

Good Fortune 35: Out-of-the-box thinking pays off.

In less than ten years HP had a full line of dot matrix printers and had introduced the LaserJet and Inkjet printers. These products dominated personal and small system printing for many years.

Boise grew rapidly and in 1976 the new Disk Memory Division was moved to Boise with Dick Hackborn as Division Manager. That same year construction of the first building on the permanent site was completed. The Boise Division played a major role in HP's enormous success in computer printers.

Growth leads to new opportunity

In September of 1974 HP announced a new group structure, bringing together all of HP's activities in the computer industry. The Computer Systems Group included the Data Systems Division in Cupertino, the Automatic Measurements Division in Sunnyvale, the Boise Division in Idaho, and the Grenoble Division in France. The new Group also consolidated all the sales, marketing and customer support. I was appointed Group General Manager. Over time the key managers in this Group came to include quite a few individuals from the Microwave Division.

By the end of 1974 the new Group organization was already improving performance, and the issues that had prompted my arrival in Cupertino were pretty well resolved. The HP Way was flourishing. People had begun to trust one another and communication between departments had improved markedly. The 2100 series was growing significantly and the 3000 performance issues were behind us, with further improvements in performance on the way.

Good Fortune 36: Once more—promotion and opportunity.

Now the Real Challenge

It had been almost two years since I had left the Microwave Division. Ten years of training there had taught me well the blocking and tackling that were fundamental to HP success and I had learned how to manage an HP Division. Helped by that training, the issues that had brought me to Cupertino were behind us. Now, however, the task at hand was more complex and difficult. There were now multiple divisions to be managed and integrated with an overarching plan and strategy.

The company, an inexperienced player in a large and rapidly expanding market, was seeking opportunity in an undefined niche that might not even exist. We were the leader in our traditional instrument business. An overarching strategy had been set and followed years earlier. A successful sales process and organization was in place.

But, in computers, we faced many larger competitors and were dwarfed by IBM. We needed to create a strategy and plan for this business and needed to create a marketing and sales organization with the policies processes and skills required to impact this market. These were challenges I had not previously faced.

Were the lessons learned and the skills acquired adequate to help me overcome these challenges? A wiser man might have hesitated or brought in an outside consultant. It just never occurred to me. Remember, "Ready, Fire, Aim."

The new group organization was a good starting point for the challenges we faced. The four division managers were all proven HP people. No outsiders were brought in to fill key positions. However, who to choose and how to organize the worldwide marketing, sales and support organization was not at all clear. For the time being I kept the existing people and organization in place. Two of the four divisions were in Cupertino, where I was located. One was focused on the technical computer products and the other on business computers. Although there were strategic questions across both divisions, the day-to-operations were well handled by the division managers. The Boise Division had been launched earlier to get HP into the computer printer business, which it did with flying colors. The Grenoble Division manufactured some of the computer products for the European market and over time developed system add-ons and enhancements.

Good Fortune 37: The opportunities keep coming!

In looking back now, each of the opportunities I faced had been unexpected; each of my jobs engrossed me and provided joy. I had no career plan—good things just happened. The self-confidence that moved me forward was, at least in part, fostered by the "good fortune" that had benefited me throughout my life. I recall on numerous occasions saying to my wife, "Barbara, I have had such a string of good luck. When will it end and when it does will there be a big price to pay?"

Needed — A Strategy and Plan for Success

Over the next couple of years most of my time was devoted to identifying and putting in place the team of managers who could create success for HP in the computer business. As the team came together, with their help we began to make progress on a strategy to guide the organization and a plan on how to implement that strategy.

We started with a situation analysis of our current status. At this point we had been designing and selling technical computers for a number of years. Digital Equipment (DEC) was the leader in this business and had a substantial lead. HP had three offerings in this area: real time systems built into the customer's products; time share systems supporting sixteen or more terminals sold to schools and more broadly to end-users for terminal access to computer capabilities; and general purpose systems sold mostly for measurement control and data collection purposes.

In business computers, we now had a product that worked and had verified specifications. However, we had little or no idea of how this product fit into the business marketplace or how to market and sell it.

In the Boise Division we had a small start in providing a printer suitable for our systems and we had begun to develop other customers for that product.

Plenty to do

This situation analysis made clear we had plenty to do. The starting point was to lay out a strategic plan for each of the three primary programs: technical computers, business computers, and peripherals. As we did so, we felt we should and could find synergies to bind all three elements together.

The peripheral piece of the strategy was the easiest. We wanted to exploit the benefits of decentralization by giving them the freedom to innovate in the peripherals (printers, storage devices, terminal and so forth) most needed in our systems. This implied a change, because previously, the computer engineers had specified all the technical details of the peripherals. Now Boise would have that responsibility. Of course they were expected to choose to do those kind of products needed by our systems. If other customers also sought their products, even competitors, it would only enhance HP's position.

The technical systems strategy was almost as simple. We knew who the potential customers were and had a sales team already selling to them quite well. Part of the strategy was to have separate sales forces for technical computers and business computers. It also recognized at some point we might need another team for peripherals. Selling technical computers involved selling to engineers using real time computers in their product or a production engineer working on controlling production equipment. Some customers might be using HP computers to interface with HP instruments where, in fact, the instruments and computers had been designed to work together. All of this led us to an industry focus on manufacturing.

Technical computers needed special strategies when the computer was embedded in the customer's product. Certain sales people in each district focused on these opportunities. The sale might start with the engineer but would eventually lead to negotiating a volume contract with a high-level officer and a purchasing executive. In HP's instrument business, we never gave discounts. So we showed the HP CFO how these volume discounts reduced our selling costs and got his approval for the program The major competitor for these products was DEC.

Known and unknown

For the business computer strategy we knew we now had a product that worked, was fully characterized, and might be attractive for some kinds of business applications. Unknown was what those business applications were, and what kind of customers might need them. We had very little information to help identify a market niche where we might be able to succeed against IBM. We had sold very few of the model 3000 business computers, but we concluded generating some orders was the best way we had to get concrete info to help solve the daunting challenge we faced.

A detour—an expensive failure

It is painful for me to report on a big and costly mistake. We had made major strides back in the Microwave Division using sapphire substrates to build microwave integrated circuits. Two of the key engineers involved believed they could develop digital integrated circuits by depositing silicon on sapphire (SOS). They predicted that this approach could provide important advantages.

I gave the go ahead and we invested in a facility to build SOS devices and demonstrate the advantages. At every step of the way we ran into obstacles that could only be overcome by further investment. It was a mistake to have launched this project at all but I made my mistake much larger and more expensive by failing to terminate it far sooner than I did.

In fact, this was an unnecessary detour. HP did not need a unique integrated circuit technology to succeed in the computer business. There were numerous semiconductor companies developing the technology and products we would need, and even if SOS had been successful, it simply would have further distracted us from where our focus needed to be.

This was a very expensive mistake—several million dollars' worth. Equally bad, some of HP's best people were tied up for a couple years striving for success. How could I have made such a big mistake?

I have puzzled over this mistake ever since. It was actually two mistakes: launching the project at all and then failing to terminate it earlier. My best guess is that it was my ego that got it started and then, because it was a distraction, I paid very little attention, combined with my ego again to avoid terminating it. But God does not favor success in endeavors driven by ego. There was a mite of good fortune in that the project was not the distraction it might have been.

Learning to Sell in an IBM World

So now I am back to the main order of business. My first step was to visit with sales people in several sales offices to get an impression of what was going on. These were not encouraging visits—not surprising, as there was a good deal of confusion. I decided it would be best to start afresh and I asked a well-regarded HP manager with both marketing and sales experience to help solve the problem.

At this point only a couple of the thirty sales people had gotten more than one order. Some had not even gotten their first order. The sales manager and I decided that we should ask each of the sales people to strive to sell one machine each quarter. Gradually over the next few months or so the sales increased. We held a general sales meeting for all of the people selling the 3000 and asked each to get up in front of everybody and tell what they had accomplished over the prior six months. Most of the increased sales had come from very few individuals. We asked them to outline for the others their sales process. As they described their process, several things became clear: they had territories with many small businesses; they often were talking to the owner when they called on possible accounts; and they rigorously qualified these prospects and quickly moved on unless it was clear there was an immediate opportunity.

The individuals attempting to sell to large companies were having the most difficulties. Even getting in to see the head of the company's computer operations was difficult and often when they did, they found him totally captive to IBM. Nonetheless, one salesperson did find opportunities for the 3000 in the large accounts at the department level or in a remote division. The problem was getting orders through the MIS manager or the executive management.

Progress from the bottom up

As a result of these findings we organized the 3000 sales force into two teams—one team selling to small businesses and the other to large companies. We asked each team to take responsibility for developing and refining a sales process for their respective parts of the market. This bottoms-up process was surprisingly rapid and effective, particularly for the small business team. The process for the small business team we called "trolling" which, over the next months, became well understood. The process for the large business team we termed "persuasion."

Trolling for success

The trolling process started with direct mail to a list of small businesses in a defined geography, usually the assigned territory of two or three sales people. The mail piece described the 3000 and at the end asked if the company had interest in this type of product. The sales people would then visit these firms to gather info and identify the decision maker. If it looked like there might be an opportunity, the key players at the companies were then invited to a "seminar" at a local hotel. Some twenty to fifty individuals would be invited, and the sales people would follow up to assure the right people came.

One or two knowledgeable individuals from the division would make the presentation of the benefits of the HP system. Both before and after the presentations there would be some refreshments to allow the HP people to chat with the potential customers. This was the "qualification" step and the team got quite good at it. The whole process up to this point was visualized as a funnel, with two or three hot prospects dropping out of the bottom after each seminar. Typically, we got an order or two in the next few weeks. Over the next couple of years the business grew rapidly as we added sales people and district managers. This process, invented by key sales people and their managers, really turned things around. The process continued to be defined and was fully documented by the team.

Good Fortune 38: A strong creative team found the answer.

Persuading—a more complicated process

Meanwhile, the sales cycle for the team calling on large accounts was much longer and the process in each account was somewhat unique. We quickly learned how to "disqualify" the accounts that were tightly centralized, usually with IBM in control of the executive in charge of decisions relating to their computers. It required that we find a "champion" at the division or department level who had an application that was not supported by the corporate systems or organization. We heavily focused on manufacturing companies and often this required that we bring in a suitable software supplier. A good example was Ask Computer, a software reseller using the 3000. They had an excellent manufacturing package. Sometimes they would bring us in and get us started in an account, and on other occasions HP would originate the sale and bring in ASK. It was a very symbiotic relationship.

Of course, our goal with these large accounts was building long-term relationships that resulted in multiple orders. It took a while, but eventually we achieved many important long-term relationships.

Good Fortune 39: Focus and teamwork led to success.

We now had the elements of our strategy and plan for business computers. Our plan was to grow the sales force and continually refine and improve the sales process, particularly for large accounts. In the sales territories a salesperson proficient at the trolling process was assigned to small accounts and a salesperson proficient in the persuasion process to only large accounts. We developed training programs for both types of sales processes.

We gained enough information from the sales process development to draft a concise five-page set of slides which set out our Goals, Strategy, and Plan for success. These slides brought together business computers, technical computers, and peripherals with a market focus on large manufacturing companies where all of our products gained synergy. It also made clear the specialized opportunities available for our business products in small businesses of all types and for technical computers used within other systems. This was an ever-evolving document driven by technology and frequent updates to the situation analysis.

Solving Constraints to Growth

However, before we could do well in this effort with either large or small companies, there were two important issues that required attention. The first was how do we find the sales people to continue the rapid growth we had begun to achieve; the second issue was how do we provide the level of support and uptime these customers all required.

In growing the sales force, we found a very limited supply of experienced sales people to hire. Many were IBM second stringers and all were very expensive. Furthermore, our experience was that many of those we did hire did not work out. Because of my experiences in recruiting engineering and marketing professionals, I put forth the idea that we night try hiring fresh college graduates. For inside jobs, that was HP's practice. The outcry against such a crazy idea was enormous. "Paul, you don't understand how different it is to build sales skills and how long it takes!" "These people will be calling on company owners or high level executives who don't want to waste their time with youngsters still wet behind the ears." But, again, a few courageous sales managers thought it might work and gave it a try. They had little to lose because the other alternatives were not providing adequate personnel.

Well, it turned out these young recruits were full of energy and creative ideas. They were fearless in trying new and different tactics. They were not constrained by their past experiences. Their success came quickly and, surprisingly, some of the older sales people learned and adopted their tactics.

Let's bring in the women!

My next step was to suggest we try women for sales openings. It took very little of my encouragement for a couple of our innovative sales managers to hire women as salespeople. Up to this point it was men only; and again, there was some resistance, but as we got started with female salespeople, the results were fantastic. In a few years, several women were among our top ten salespeople. It did not take long for a woman to win the award for top salesperson. I can still picture the scene when she received that award in front of all the top sales performers and their management.

Good Fortune 40: : Success by defying conventional wisdom

Eliminating the IBM support advantage

We now had the processes and people to grow sales, but we were bumping up against the second major obstacle limiting our growth. Our computers were increasingly being used in mission critical applications. If our product was down in any way, even for a short time, our customer's business was affected. They expected our product to function at all times. In some cases, this meant 24/7. In others cases, it meant any interruption of any kind during the workday. In large companies, IBM would have legions of support people and resources on site. Even in small companies, IBM offices would be close by. IBM was more than ten times the size of HP, and convincing our customers that we could match IBM in keeping their computers up and running seemed like an overwhelming obstacle. This issue was understandably limiting our growth. We could not overcome this obstacle with superior marketing or a sales presentation. It required more than words; we needed proven results.

Step one was to focus on the reliability of our systems. This was not a new effort as HP had been striving for superior quality and reliability in its products for a number of years. Reliable computers required outstanding quality in both the hardware and software. To the extent we could exceed the reliability of IBM's products, their advantage in manpower was reduced. Our efforts for superior reliability in the computer group were reemphasized and strengthened. Our products were already well recognized for quality and reliability, and the engineering and manufacturing teams achieved remarkable further improvements over the next twenty-four months.

Good Fortune 41: Industry leading reliability.

In parallel, we focused on building a world-class support team. Several key managers were transferred to lead the support organization. They hired outstanding people and trained and equipped them well. They began innovating in numerous ways to reduce the IBM advantage in headcount. For example, they concluded that if we got the customer set up and started properly, it minimized future problems. This included working up front with the sales people to make sure the system was properly configured and could meet the customer's expectations. Comprehensive training of the customer at the start was essential, as was top-quality help to get the system set up and performing properly. We increased reliability by assuring the mass memory system was adequately backed up, or "mirrored." These front end investments paid off handsomely.

The speed and insight with which the support organization devised new strategies and organized to carry them out seemed to flow like magic. There were a few key players at every level who brought this about.

Good Fortune 42: Again, an extraordinary team effort.

Of course, not everything proceeded perfectly. Mistakes were made, but they were recognized quickly and corrected. Many innovations were created to overcome the IBM size advantage. But one of the most effective of these came when HP guaranteed "uptime" for its computers. Uptime was a measure used by many customers and was defined as the percent of the total time the customer contracted to have their machine(s) running and fully functional. When this program was initiated, the guarantee was ninety-eight percent uptime and, as the program matured, we were able to increase that percentage. The customers loved it and it was quite rare that it was not achieved. In the late '70s, HP received the JD Power award for the best support in the computer industry. This was quite an achievement by the people in HP's support organization and propelled the ongoing growth of HP computers. Support was no longer a growth constraint.

Good Fortune 43: Bold ambition pays off!

Promoting the strategy

We originated five strategy slides when the strategy and plan were just beginning to be refined. With the help of the group's top managers, we kept refining the five slides that concisely laid out the strategic focus, current status, and plans and objectives for the year ahead, as well as the longer-term future. These slides were always with me and I used every opportunity to present them to the HP people wherever I went—sales offices, divisions throughout the company, corporate groups—up, down, and everywhere. The purpose for doing this was to make sure as many people as possible knew where we were heading and what we wanted to accomplish. This knowledge gave everyone the opportunity to contribute to the goals. At the very least it got everyone pointed in the same direction.

The manufacturing industry remained our primary strategic focus for many years, but companies in other industries heard about our products and capabilities and quite a few became customers. Individual large account sales people (the "persuaders") focused on manufacturing companies, but when they had time, would check out other large potential accounts in their territory. Think about a major account person in Manhattan. There were few manufacturing concerns, primarily corporate headquarters, and lots and lots of large financial institutions. We gradually began to build up knowledge in this area, and they became a secondary market focus. Our strategy slides illustrated the slowly broadening market interest.

Succeeding in the international arena

The computer sales and support organization were also performing well in international markets. As these strategies for growth got started in the U.S., the international leaders came often for sales and marketing meetings. They adopted the plans rapidly and soon were contributing ideas and innovations to the U.S. teams. Europe had a very strong computer sales team and was not even one step behind in carrying out the strategy. They rapidly adapted the sales and marketing strategies to the local environment. Outside Europe and in smaller countries, the sales team was managed by the country organization and successfully adapted the U.S. strategy as appropriate. The Australian organization was particularly successful. International sales were a big part of our success.

Of course the Grenoble Division, as part of the computer organization, was able to provide direct support quickly. I asked Cyril Yansouni from the Microwave Division to head up the

Grenoble Division. Cyril and his wife spoke fluent French. She was born in Belgium and Cyril who grew up in Egypt had been sent to Belgium to attend university there. Then he came to Stanford for a PhD. In the Microwave Division I had recruited Cyril from Stanford. He had completed all course work for his PhD and had only a thesis to write; he never got the chance. In a few years I asked Cyril and his wife to move to Santa Rosa for the Microwave Division. Now later, for HP computers, I went to Santa Rosa and asked Cyril to move to France. Then, after several years in Grenoble, I asked him to come back to California to be a top executive in the computer organization. These were not easy moves for Cyril's wife but each time after a few tears she gathered herself and went forward with the move.

Growth and Change

In parallel with the development of HP's computer sales and support capabilities, the division engineering organizations had continued to expand and improve the product offering. Likewise, during this time, the division manufacturing organizations had made continuous improvements in product cost and quality, as well as reducing days of inventory. There were notable expense reductions throughout the administrative organizations, as well. Taken together, these factors fostered continued and meaningful growth in revenue and profit. By 1980, the computer groups had grown to almost fifty percent of the total Hewlett Packard Company.

Good Fortune 44: We were "firing on all cylinders."

Through the '60s and early '70s, the HP Instrument Group was by far the dominant HP business, and the company policies and organization reflected this. Then, as the computer business gained scale and prominence, new policies and structures came into place. This was most pronounced in the sales and support organizations all over the world. Quite often, computers and instruments were sold to the same companies. However, the instrument selling was done engineer to engineer in the labs and production while the computers were sold to the top-level managers and company officers. These changes were disruptive and frustrating to the people in HP's instrument business. At some point in the late '70s, the Hewlett Packard Company classification by Wall Street was changed from an instrument company to a computer company. This did not help the situation in any way and only increased the friction within the company. It also did not help that the press and financial community focused all their attention on HP's computer business, and frequently on me, personally. I received many requests for press interviews. Of course I enjoyed the attention, but it became increasingly awkward and embarrassing. To make matters worse, when our CEO, John Young, and I would go to New York for analysts' meetings, I would be asked most of the questions and, after our presentations, would have a large gang of analysts surrounding me.

In 1977 I was elected an HP Vice President, reflecting the growing size and importance of the computer groups. Then, in 1980, I was elected Executive Vice President, a member of the executive committee, and a member of the Hewlett Packard Board of Directors. You can be sure I was honored by that recognition. Shortly thereafter, John Young, then President and CEO, asked me to move my office from Cupertino where I had been since that day more than seven years earlier when I had been sent there to resolve the troubles in HP's computer business.

Good Fortune 45: Great recognition-unexpected trials.

Life in the den of corporate top management

Within a short interval I was settled in my attractive new office in the corporate headquarters surrounded by the other three Executive Vice Presidents and the CEO. This turned out to be a far more dramatic change than I had expected. First of all, I was immediately immersed in a range of corporate activities that occupied almost half of my time. Some of them were informal, occurring because I was only a few feet away from the other executive officers. But many activities were formally scheduled and/or involved travel to other company operations unrelated to the computer business. By this time, the computer group was quite large, with four or five group managers reporting to me each managing a number of divisions. There were a dozen or more divisions, some growing very rapidly. In my former Cupertino office I could walk in a few minutes to most of the group managers who were the center of my business contacts. My new corporate level responsibilities kept me far busier and were more distracting than I expected.

Personal Computers—a lost opportunity

IBM, Apple, and others had introduced so-called personal computers over several years prior to 1980. However, none had made any major impact; but two things occurred that were destined to have major impacts. The first occurred at Xerox Parc in Palo Alto. In 1979 the team at Xerox invited several companies to come to their labs to see their Star computer with a revolutionary graphical interface. HP was one of the companies invited. John Young and I attended their presentation. It was very exciting. We had been exploring the possibilities of converting one of the terminals developed for the 3000 computers into a personal computer. If you have read the book *Steve Jobs* by Walter Isaacson you know that Apple and Steve had also been invited to Xerox Parc and saw that demo. It had a profound effect, and Apple introduced the Macintosh Computer, embodying much of that graphical interface, a few years later.

The second thing was the introduction in 1981 of the IBM 5150, named a personal computer. That introduction truly launched the personal computer industry. It had no graphical user interface but many companies rushed to copy what IBM had done. It used Microsoft DOS software that was very unfriendly. It took years for Microsoft to provide a graphical user interface.

Several of the key people in the computer organization wanted, as I did, to develop a machine based on the Xerox graphical user interface (GUI). We had the talent to do it. Under development at the time was the Amigo project that included a GUI. The Amigo was a large, heavy, roll around machine costing over ten thousand dollars. It never went anywhere but would have been a huge help in creating a GUI-based PC. In fact, one of the engineers working on that team left to join Apple and do just that.

John Young felt we were falling behind in our minicomputer processor technology and did not want us to be distracted. He suggested we proceed with an IBM clone.

Had HP chosen to innovate rather than just following IBM, the company role and success in the PC industry might have been different. However, to provide the resources and people to do that and not detract from our other programs would have required the Amigo program be completely redirected. In retrospect that would have been a wise decision but I did not make it. This decision to do a "me-to clone" was so unlike the HP I had grown up in. But, unlike my normal questioning and outspoken behavior, I just went along with John's suggestion peacefully in my new role as a corporate executive.

You will see after I left HP, I had another opportunity to do the kind of personal computer that would shake the industry. But I failed to grasp that opportunity as well and this time all on my own!

The Perils of Paul ... In Top Management

In addition to my new corporate activities, there was an even more disconcerting change in the management situation. John Young had become committed to what was referred to as "management by consensus." To implement this process, John, with help from others, adopted what was called the rows and columns management system. The idea was to bring into a single project team individuals from different functional parts of the organization. I won't go into all the details of this concept, but the result for me was not good. This process required lots of meetings frequently quite large. To me the decision overhead was overwhelming.

This consensus management process was frustratingly slow and did not seem to fit well with the rapidly evolving computer business. My impatience left me increasingly frustrated and my rapid decision making style was not useful in this environment. It was certainly quite different from the approach I had learned at HP and had practiced throughout my career.

John and others felt that the growth and size of the company required the consensus approach to coordinate the wide range of activities now necessary to develop and market computer systems. It was clearly not an environment for which I was well suited. Add to this the fact that the time I had available to manage the computer business—whatever the process—was limited by the schedule of corporate activities. John asserted himself and wanted to be personally involved in all major decisions to assure consensus had been reached. This scene was totally at odds with my earlier relationship with John.

In addition to these issues, I found myself also occasionally at odds with the other members of the executive committee. The executive committee consisted of three EVPs who ran the company's operations and an EVP responsible for Corporate Administration and Finance—five people, including John the CEO. In general the decisions made by the executive committee were excellent and I was proud to be part of that group

One of the meetings though typified the situations where I was at odds with the others. John had asked the HR manager to analyze the HP benefits situation. Well, HR prepared a comprehensive report that compared HP's benefits to a number of other Silicon Valley companies, as well as technology companies located elsewhere. The HR manager finished his report by stating that we were in very good shape because HP's benefits were "right at the average."

The other four executives expressed satisfaction with this result. I expressed great disappointment with the result and their reaction. I felt that their satisfaction was unlike the company I had been part of for the past twenty years. The HP I knew had never settled for average in anything it did, not for its products, not for the respect and trust it held for its employees, not for its commitment to customers and suppliers, not for its performance expectations. HP was considered an exceptional company. Its people felt they worked for an exceptional company, as I did. The others explained to me, "We've grown too big to have exceptional benefits." They may have been right but it seemed to me out of character for the company I so respected.

And now the coup de grace

What was going on? Here I was at the ultimate point of a wonderful career and the things that had so shaped and guided me were melting away around me. What happened to trust, individual leadership, responsibility, and accountability for results? With the committee structure, who was responsible; who was accountable? Leadership creates consensus, not committee meetings. (I have been told Dave Packard came back to the company in 1989 and changed some of what I found so frustrating. I was not there so I can't vouch for that as the truth)

Then came the ultimate disappointment. John Young engaged McKinsey Consulting in a project to review the HP organization. This was atypical since HP rarely used consulting companies at all, much less for such a sweeping topic. I met the people from McKinsey at the project start but was not involved with them after that. They developed a sweeping proposal that, as John explained to me, accomplished two important objectives. First, it made it possible to present the company's full capabilities to our customers by combining computer and instrument sales and support organizations. Second, it introduced more of the company's top management to involvement in the computer business. This second objective did make some sense to me. At that point computers were more than fifty percent of the company's sales and employees. For the past twelve years, none of the other top executives had any computer experience. Two new executive vice presidents were appointed to split the computer factory operations and they reported to a new chief operating officer. All of those appointed were quite capable people not previously involved in HP's computer business. The extra talent and new COO clearly solved the problem I was having dividing my time between managing the computer business and the new corporate responsibilities.

On the other hand, I believed combining the sales organizations would prove to be a major mistake. The computer sales and support organization was many times larger than the instrument sales organization, had necessarily different policies, sold to high-level executives, and had very different sales processes. I have already outlined how much effort and time it had taken to develop HP's unique and winning sales processes. The differences in support were equally dramatic. Computers had onsite 24/7 support with guaranteed uptime vs. the Instrument Division's "Bring it in and we'll have it for you in a few days." It had taken many years to identify, train, and put in place the individuals to manage the computer sales and support organizations. The thought of disrupting that operation and putting in place new managers with little or no knowledge of how and why the organization functioned as it did upset me greatly

Furthermore, it was extremely disappointing that John had decided to completely remove me from any role in HP's computer business. To say the least, to me, this did seem unjust and unwise. Why was the person who had spent more than a decade managing HP's growth and success as a computer company no longer involved in even an advisory role in that business?

I was extremely disconcerted, which I expressed to John Young, along with my opinion on the likely outcome of the newly combined sales and support organizations. John listened and then countered that he had thought this through and it had been presented and approved by the board.

My new assignment was to take responsibility for the company's three smaller businesses: Medical, Analytical, and Components. I chose to take on my new assignment with good cheer and complained to no one. I did not take my concerns about the sales organization to Dave Packard. I realized later that might have been a mistake.

I had reported directly to John for almost my entire career at HP, with only a few short exceptions. John had been a huge help to me over the years and had guided my development and career. I had always truly enjoyed working for him. He could see that I was frustrated and not doing well adapting to the new consensus management, committee-oriented structure. It also must have been obvious to him that the extensive demands on my time for "corporate tasks" left me little time to manage the company's largest and most complex business. My long and positive relationship with John had deteriorated in major ways.

I was further hurt that John had planned these changes over a period of several months without once discussing his plans with me. He clearly had done everything necessary to make this a fait accompli before he told me. This was uncharacteristic of my prior relationship with John. Although I was aware that John was not happy with my performance at this point, I felt unjustly treated by the changes and by the process used. To this day I do not know why John did this, and in this way. He did not tell me the reason.

Nonetheless, I am indebted to John for all the help, guidance, and opportunity he provided throughout my career at Hewlett Packard. Without that help from John, my success would have been far more limited.

Good Fortune 46: Not so much good, but part of God's plan.

In reflecting back now as I write this, it is likely that my change of fortune was part of God's plan for me. No one could design circumstances more certain to frustrate and defeat me than those that I faced at this time in my career. All that I had learned about leadership, accountability, and delegation was of little use to me. These circumstances played to my biggest weakness—impatience for action. After all the good fortune of my years prior to being promoted to top management, I was now facing a new type of lesson. It was time to be trained in Humility and Patience. Of course, at the time, I knew nothing of God and His presence in my life, so my reaction was hurt feelings, sadness, and confusion.

I am not sure how John expected me to react when he told me. I simply accepted his decision as gracefully as I could. I did not resist in any way, did not go to either Bill or Dave to state my case or to try to change things. In fact, I complained to no one, not even my wife. I think John might have thought I would blow up and quit on the spot, but I simply turned to my new responsibilities. I did nothing to impede the change or make it more difficult. When people came to me expressing concern, I did my best to set them at ease and asked them to do their best to make the new organization successful. I received many compliments for my behavior in the situation from people all over the company.

Certainly I was heartbroken, particularly with the plight of the sales team that we had built, and concerned for the people who I had selected and promoted to key jobs. I feared many would be pushed aside and their careers would be threatened. In spite of my disappointment, I did not consider leaving the company. I loved Hewlett Packard and it had been very good to me. So, for the next several months, I put my head down and focused on my new assignment.

Confusion reigns

I started into my new assignment with good intent and submerged my disappointment and confusion about why I had been so completely removed from the business I had been building for the past twelve years. I now had responsibility for three operating groups plus the corporate research labs. The operating groups were the Medical Group that developed, built, and sold medical instrumentation systems primarily to hospitals; the Analytical Group that developed, built, and sold chemical and material measurement systems for use in a wide variety of companies (including the semiconductor industry); and the Components Group that developed, manufactured, and sold light emitting diodes and other solid-state components. The corporate research lab had been quite important to the company in all of its businesses. This was an assignment I should have been delighted with, but the excitement was gone and my heart was elsewhere. The confusion over why I found myself in this situation was sabotaging my good intent.

In any case, in spite of my lack of enthusiasm, I went forward in my new assignment. I proceeded as usual: talking with the key people in each group to find out what was going on and to determine where I might be of some help.

As you might guess, this was a big deal throughout the high tech and computer industry. Within a day I started getting calls from headhunters, venture capitalists, and a variety of companies. I had been receiving such calls over the past years, but nothing like this onslaught. At this point I simply continued my past practice—that was to say I was not interested in leaving HP. After a few months, still suffering my disillusionment and lack of enthusiasm, I concluded that some of the opportunities brought to my attention sounded pretty interesting and I should probably listen.

Time to Leave?

Before I did agree to talk with anyone though, I went to see Dave and told him that I was going to look at some other companies. He responded by asking that before I made any commitments I come back to see him. So I started listening.

Over the next two or three months, I checked out a few situations. Several venture partnerships invited me to join as a partner, and/or had companies they wanted me to look at. But I was only fifty-two and I reasoned I could still join a venture firm in five or ten years if that seemed appropriate. There were several interesting opportunities, but I ruled out anything outside the Bay Area. I talked with board members and key executives at several companies but always there were issues, frequently a founder, to be dealt with.

Then, in December, a company came to my attention that intrigued me. It had been the darling of Silicon Valley for several years but was now reportedly headed for bankruptcy. This company, Convergent Technologies, had the highest growth rate in the U.S. for the past year but did not have the ability to cope with that growth. Given my HP training, this seemed an opportunity to me and, as I looked, three things intrigued me.

First, the company had a very unique and successful workstation product line. These networked workstations were a mainstay of Burroughs's primary business with banks. Convergent had major long-term contracts for this product. Second, they had a very large development and initial production contract with AT&T to create a Unix-based PC with a graphical user interface. The user interface was based on the Xerox Parc technology, which the Apple Mac was based on. This was a fully integrated PC with a built-in display. When I visited the company for interviews I saw an early prototype and met the team responsible. I was overwhelmed! This was the type of thing I had wanted to do at HP. WOW!

Finally, I met a few key people and was impressed. Two of the seven founding employees I knew from HP. Much of The HP Way had taken hold there and was combined with an impatience to achieve. The San Jose *Mercury News* referred to Convergent as the "Marine Corps of Silicon Valley." This was truly an intriguing situation.

Christmas was approaching so I decided to ponder the situation over the holidays during our normal family skiing vacation. I requested and brought with me to Colorado the detailed company financial statements. An analysis of these convinced me that roughly one hundred million dollars could be rescued from the balance sheet to pay off the banks and fund the company.

Just before Christmas I met with the founder and CEO. He literally begged me to come in and save the company. He promised to disappear from the company, resign from the board and give me lots of money and lots of stock. The headhunter who had brought me to this situation offered to introduce me to Larry Sonsini, the head of the most prestigious law firm in the Valley to handle the negotiations with both Convergent and HP. Before I left for the family get-together, I met with Larry and briefed him on my situation at HP, provided copies of all my HP options, my salary, and other perks.

Half-way through the holiday in Colorado, this situation seemed more than just intriguing, so it was time to see if Larry could put something together that would recover the value of unvested HP options and other financial benefits which would be left behind. He got close and it seemed best to return home before New Year's to determine if agreement could be achieved. Right after New Year's, Larry had something I could accept.

Final discussion with Dave

Before making a final commitment I went to see Dave Packard. Leaving Hewlett Packard was one of the most difficult things I have ever done. I told him I had found something interesting and intended to leave the company. What Dave then said to me was confusing and unexpected; it affected me greatly. All I can do now is repeat what I believe I heard. He said, "Paul, some time ago we choose John as our CEO. Had we waited, things might have been different (for you). We feel now is not the time to change that."

Part of what he said was ambiguous. The first statement was a fact but what did Dave mean when he said "Had we waited things might have been different (for you)?" It seemed so positive it hit me emotionally, but I can never be sure what he truly meant. Possibly it was just Dave's way of saying they thought highly of me. At the end he made clear this was not the time to question John's authority

Dave went on to tell me how sorry he was that I found myself in this situation and they understood why I had decided to leave. As I left Dave's office my eyes were so full of tears I could hardly find my car. I sobbed all the way home.

This conversation took place more than twenty-five years ago. I have thought about it often since then. I can't be absolutely certain that what I carried home with me that day is correct. But in all the intervening years my reaction has remained unchanged.

Good Fortune 47: An important new insight.

I now believe that I should never have left HP. My lessons in humility and patience had just begun. Had I remained at HP in my new role, that training would have intensified and continued. I longed to stay at HP but my pride and ego were in control. I bailed out on the lessons God wanted to teach me. I left that special company, thereby avoiding the training God had prepared for me. We are each granted free will but there are consequences for what we choose. Never again did I experience the amazing success and fulfillment that accompanied my years at HP. No one knows what would have transpired had I stayed and followed God's plan, but I am confident it would have been far different.

CHAPTER 4

Business Life After HP

Now - Convergent Technologies

My first days at Convergent were similar to my first days at HP's Computer Division—I went around talking one-on-one with lots of people, attempting to understand the situation and the people. As before, I knew very few of them. As I listened, again, I heard far more than the actual words that were spoken.

Good Fortune 48: God's grace had not fully departed.

Good fortune also remained with me in the form of Geri Cherem. My invaluable secretary for the prior seventeen years at HP had agreed to come with me to Convergent. Leaving HP was a big step for Geri. She gave up her position and security in a wonderful company. Convergent's founder offered to provide her with a significant "signing bonus." You can imagine how important it was for me to have someone who knew me so well and who I could trust completely.

It was very positive to find first-class engineering and manufacturing teams. Quickly it became obvious that most of the problems leading the company toward bankruptcy were in the finance and marketing parts of the company. The symptoms were excess accounts receivable and inventory, but the causes were setting delivery schedules, prices, and in some cases, performance specs by marketing without the concurrence of manufacturing or engineering. The chief marketing officer believed he had the authority to commit prices and delivery schedules to customers and then inform manufacturing what was required of them. Customers were not paying because of late deliveries and/or performance issues. Certain contracts were priced in a manner that made profit almost impossible.

My next step was a heart-to-heart with the head of marketing. When he learned that he no longer had the authority to set prices, delivery schedules, and performance specifications, he was very unhappy. This was a long and contentious meeting, but he finally understood. Pricing data was from finance and if the sales or contract price he wanted would result in less than twenty percent profit, he needed my approval. Likewise, delivery commitments came from manufacturing, and performance specs from engineering. As with prices, any deviation in quotes or contracts needed my approval.

After a couple of meetings with the finance head, I concluded he was part of the problem and needed to be replaced. There did not appear to be anybody in the finance organization capable of replacing him. This was a key job and it was going to be very hard to find and hire a competent replacement quickly. However, good fortune again intervened to solve that problem. Before I was able to hire a headhunter I received a call from John Russell, co-controller for HP. John had been my financial guru ever since I had first become engineering manager twenty years earlier. He told me he was disappointed because I hadn't called him to come help at Convergent. He knew the current Convergent CFO from various meetings of financial professionals and was sure I would not be satisfied with him. In two weeks my "hurt" friend was at work in the office next to me.

Even before John Russell called me I had made a firm decision not to actively recruit HP employees. Over time, though, similar to John, a number of individuals called concerning their desire to leave HP. Many of these did end up working at Convergent and made important contributions.

One of these was Cyril Yansouni, a top manager in HP's Computer Organization whom I wrote about earlier in the book. He became the president of Convergent. When I arrived at Convergent, I found a culture much like that at HP. Two of Convergent's founders had been from HP and, clearly, their culture had won out. Thankfully, the presence of a few more HP alumni in the organization helped strengthen this culture without diminishing the unique Convergent penchant for action.

We delayed the yearend financial report several weeks till John, now CFO, and I could review the books. We wrote off anything questionable and started working on recovering the cash from the bloated balance sheet. Using the business basics my new CFO, the manufacturing manager, and I all had learned at HP, we had cash in the bank and were profitable by summer. In a year we had almost $100 million cash surplus. Once the business basics were in place, manufacturing and finance set out to build world-class organizations on which they made steady progress.

At that point I turned my attention to engineering and the product opportunities. There were three independent engineering departments. The largest of these focused on the workstation product line being sold to Burroughs. The second engineering department was responsible for the Unix workstation being developed for AT&T. And finally there was a group working on general-purpose Unix-based minicomputers.

The team developing workstations for Burroughs was very competent. They continually made valuable enhancements to that product line. Within a month of arrival at Convergent I was asked to come to the Burroughs Corporate headquarters in Detroit to meet with the CEO, Mike Blumenthal (former Secretary of the Treasury). He pressed us for major price concessions. He then announced that they would exercise their rights in the original contract to manufacture the product if we did not agree to dramatically lower our prices. This was a very contentious meeting for my first contact with Convergent's largest customer. Mike Blumenthal threatened that, with their "superior manufacturing skills," they would soon not need Convergent at all! Over the next four years this proved to be a boast that cost their company a lot of money and lost business. Unisys made major investments in a large manufacturing facility in New Jersey that never came close to matching Convergent's capabilities. Their costs were higher than Convergent's price to them. Their quality and scheduling problems created major customer problems causing a mini revolt in the Burroughs sales force.

We informed them the contract only provided rights to the original design, not the newer, enhanced design their customers wanted. Again they boasted that their engineering would solve this problem in short order. They never did, and spent a lot of money trying. They ended up closing their factory. This product line created about one billion dollars a year in sales for Burroughs and was a major profit contributor. Burroughs finally solved their problem—four years later, after a year or more of periodic meetings with Mike Blumenthal where the idea of Burroughs acquiring Convergent was always on the table. They made an offer to buy Convergent that we could not refuse.

Opportunities missed?

The team developing the Unix-based PC for AT&T was making rapid progress when I arrived at Convergent. In 1986 we started shipping products to AT&T. The contract included a start-up production run of four hundred units. These were supposed to launch the AT&T marketing program. There was no AT&T marketing program. I'm not sure they ever sold a single unit. This was a huge disappointment.

I went to New Jersey to meet with Bob Allen, the AT&T CEO at that time. I asked if he would give us a license to make and market the product. It used a proprietary AT&T processor chip and of course AT&T was already licensing the Unix software. The graphical user interface had been developed by Convergent but had been paid for by AT&T. Bob Allen did agree to give us a license to build and market the product and turned me over to negotiate a deal with the AT&T attorneys. AT&T may not have had capable marketing people but they had attorneys galore. After many weeks of negotiations, the best deal we could get resulted in license fees that were far too high—about equal to the manufacturing cost.

The Unix PC was quite similar to the iMac that Steve Jobs came up with when he returned to Apple in the late '90s. It was ten years earlier than Apple's iMac. I should have immediately launched a major effort to develop a Convergent version of the Unix workstation using commercially available Unix and commercially available chips. We had the team in place that had developed the graphical user interface for AT&T and they could do another version for Convergent. Here was the product I had wanted to do at HP with the people, resources, and know-how available to do it! Why did I fail to seize this opportunity?

There were three reasons. First, we had started purchasing small business software companies to combine with our Unix minicomputers. We believed we could build a large successful business in that market. We had already bought two companies. Even though these first steps were not encouraging, I chose to continue with that plan. We could not do both. This was another case of stubbornly sticking with a plan that showed signs of weakness.

Second, at that point, our stock price was up and the security analysts were favoring us. To do the Unix PC we would be making large investments for six or more quarters with dramatic reduction to our profits, possibly even losing money. I was committed to the small business strategy, which we would need to give up. Did I not have enough self-confidence or courage to take on those pressures? Was I enjoying all the attention and positive press too much?

Third, there were quite possibly legal challenges from AT&T's huge team of attorneys. If they came after us, it could be very costly and lead to disaster.

This was a fabulous opportunity that I would have enthusiastically pursued at HP. This might have been a very big mistake. But not the only one I made at Convergent. A year earlier Convergent had an agreement to merge with 3Com in a merger of equals. Bill Krause, the CEO of 3Com, and I knew each other and had concluded that the merged company would be a much more powerful company than the two separately. At the time of this agreement, the AT&T contract was a major positive; there was no indication that AT&T could not put together a reasonable marketing program.

In a transaction like this, investment bankers and attorneys surrounded us like a pack of wolves. 3Com's investment banker decided he could get a little better deal for his side by refusing to sign the required fairness opinion. His logic was the risks of having so much of our business depend on just two large customers. He would sign the fairness opinion if we agreed to increase the equity 3Com would receive by two or three percent. I stubbornly refused. Probably a major mistake based on what I knew then. On the other hand, if I had agreed and then the AT&T contract folded, it might have created a legal mess. So, possibly, my stubborn behavior had rescued us from a big disaster.

Good Fortune 49: Not so sure?

My caution, lack of confidence, and stubbornness were uncharacteristic of my years at HP. What was going on here? Why did I not take on these challenges? Was God no longer providing good fortune? Or was He protecting me from possible bad outcomes of these two ventures? It seems likely that both were true. I had departed from His plan and I was more on my own. But He did protect me from possible disasters. Can't be sure.

At the bargaining table

Finally, after several years of wrangling, Unisys came up with a price eighty percent above our current market price. Our workstation product line marketed by Unisys had continued to grow and was almost the only part of their computer product line doing so. Cyril and I decided to see if we could negotiate a suitable acquisition agreement. Shareholders would be happy: the offer price was sixty percent or more above the market. The major issue was the treatment of Convergent employees, particularly layoffs and stock options. We ended up with a transaction that delighted and suitably rewarded our employees.

Mike Blumenthal asked that Cyril, as Convergent president, and I remain with the Unisys organization at least through the integration period. I was appointed Executive Vice President and to the board of directors. Cyril was appointed a Unisys Vice-President and head of the former Convergent organizations. He gave us both favorable employment contracts.

In addition, Unisys made available to me the use of a Gulf Stream for my business travel. What a *seductive* benefit this was. I came to the conclusion that corporate jets can make problems for American business. They isolate executives from the real travel world that their employees must contend with.

Life interferes with business

The merger took place in January 1989. In June of that year my wife and I went to a program at the Pritikin Institute in Los Angles. This involved complete physical testing and analysis. One of the doctors told me I would die early if I did not make major changes in my lifestyle quickly. His prescription: reduce my work stress, get much more exercise, eat better and lose forty or fifty pounds. This was a two-week program and before the end, I called Mike Blumenthal and explained why I was resigning.

I also had a second reason. Barbara had been formally diagnosed with Alzheimer's two years earlier and I wanted to spend more time with her while she could enjoy it. I decided to make no other commitments for now. So I spent July with her at home and then in August we went to Istanbul where she had been born. We visited all the famous sites she remembered and tried to find the house where she had been born. We did not find the home but did visit the university where her father had taught while she lived there. After our trip to Turkey, Barbara and I went on a luxurious cruise through the Greek islands and then through the Corinth canal to Dubrovnik, Yugoslavia, and ended in Venice, Italy. We had a wonderful time. Barbara had not lost her social graces to Alzheimer's and was able to enjoy everything.

The Obligatory Venture Capital Stint

After returning from traveling with my wife in September, I became a partner in the venture capital firm Alpha Venture Partners. There were three other partners, two of who had been CEOs in other technology companies. Quickly I concluded that I could not participate full-time at the partnership—I had too many other responsibilities. First of all, of course, there was Barbara—it had become unsafe for her to drive or even be left at home alone. Second, helping my sons in their new business venture was taking quite a bit of time. Finally, I was also on the board of several public companies in addition to the venture boards my partners expected me to handle. Things got very busy again very quickly.

Fortunately, once again, Geri had volunteered to come with me to Alpha Partners. Not only was Geri helping me on all the things noted in the above paragraph, she also took on major responsibilities for helping me with Barbara. When the partners agreed with my decision to only work half time on partnership affairs, it seemed best to move to a separate office. I found a nice place in downtown Menlo Park less than ten minutes from the Alpha Office. It was no problem attending the frequent meetings at Alpha.

Before we move on to my work with Alpha, I had an earlier introduction to the venture business. In 1970 or '71 I was invited to join a group called Page Mill Partners. Page Mill was formed right in the very early years of venture capital in Silicon Valley. Jack Melchor had set it up to advise a venture investment firm he had organized in 1969. Jack had been an entrepreneur and sold the semiconductor company he had founded to HP. Jack remained at HP for a couple of years and then left and started the venture firm. It was quite an elite group Jack recruited to act as advisors and/or board members for the companies he invested in. Here are some of the members: Bob Noyce (Intel), Less Hogan (Fairchild),

John Freidenrich (Ware and Freidenrich), Ken Oshman (Rolm), John Young (HP). How I was included in such a renowned group of entrepreneurs and executives I have no idea. They were all far more accomplished than me.

Almost every one of the Page Mill members was working full-time so our partnership meetings were in the evening. We would research the companies that Jack was interested in on our own time. If Jack decided to invest in a company, each of us was free to invest alongside him. From time to time he would ask one of us to serve on the board of companies we had invested in. All this was excellent experience for me in many ways and over time provided some good financial returns.

Good Fortune 50: Meeting frequently with exceptional men.

What a fantastic learning experience. The perspectives these men expressed as we discussed possible investments, or the progress and prospects for companies in which we had earlier invested, provided long-term value throughout my career.

So now let me describe my eight active years with Alpha. Wally Davis had founded the partnership after many years in the venture business. Wally was ten years older than the rest of us. The other partners all had recent experience running successful companies. Alpha was a "seed" investor, providing the initial funding for entrepreneurs. This I particularly enjoyed. The partnership had been underway for almost two years when I joined but had just finished raising cash for a new fund. They asked me to join a couple company boards that they had funded earlier and that by this point might need two or three other VCs on the board.

We partners at Alpha would each read five or more proposals each week and then meet weekly to discuss them. We would also hear presentations from a few we had invited with interesting proposals. We might have to go through twenty or thirty proposals before we found one we liked enough to carry out a full in-depth investigation, and we would choose to invest in only a few of those.

One of us would serve on the board for any in which we invested. One such investment was particularly enjoyable. Two young men came to Alpha, one of whom I knew from HP. They had ideas for a small, inexpensive network product. Alpha liked the young men and their ideas and put up the seed money. It started with just the two of them and me as board chairman. Over the next months they made great progress. The product was introduced in about a year and follow-up products were underway. The company, Network Peripherals, went public in a few years and made quite a bit of money for Alpha. I had recruited several strong board members for the company and about a year after it went public, I resigned from the board.

My involvement included several other Alpha investments and continuing to serve on boards. Some of these other investments produced modest returns, but typical venture investing results in many failures. By 1995, Alpha had invested all the funds and had distributed the returns from successful companies. A few years latter the partnership was dissolved.

Several more public company boards had asked me to join their boards. Helping my sons in their business kept me busy and we were about to make an investment in a sailboat manufacturing company.

Public Company Boards

As Hewlett Packard prospered and I became more visible, other public companies began to be interested in me as a board member. Over the next twenty-five years I served on the boards of eight public companies, including Chairman for three at some point. Here is the list:

Hewlett Packard

In 1980 elected to the Hewlett Packard board of directors — quite an honor.

Parker Hannifin

Joined the board in 1983, revenues were just over one billion. Remained on the board for nineteen years and retired in 2002 at the age of seventy. During that time the company grew at an average rate of close to ten percent annually, quite remarkable in a consolidating industry.

Convergent Technologies

In 1985 I joined Convergent and was elected Chairman of the Board.

Spectra Physics

Joined the board of Spectra Physics in 1985 Spectra was a leader in the field of laser devices and one of the early innovators in that technology. Ciba-Geigy acquired Spectra in July 1987 in an unfriendly takeover.

Unisys

In 1989 when Unisys acquired Convergent, I became a member of that board but resigned six months later.

ASK Computer:

In 1990 joined this board. Sandy Kurtzig was the company founder and had worked with HP computers to get the company started in the mid 1970s. In 1992 Kurtzig retired. Her replacement did not perform well and was terminated by the board two years later. The board asked Bob Waterman and me to take charge and sell the company. With the help of Larry Sonsini we did so in1994.

Larry Sonsini had played an important role in my career since my resignation from Hewlett Packard. The search firm that recruited me to Convergent Technologies to negotiate my employment contract had hired him. Larry was the head of the largest and most successful legal firm in Silicon Valley providing legal services to the venture capital and growth business. He joined the Convergent board at my request. His firm helped my sons get their business started, he negotiated the sale of Convergent to Unisys, and his lawyers represented Alpha Partners. He was a board member at Ask Computer. The businesses in Silicon Valley owe a great deal to Larry and his firm.

Tektronix:

Joined the board in1992. This was a fascinating and very valuable experience. It became one of the most effective boards that I served on. There were only seven or eight members during the period I was on it. All of them were strong contributors. I resigned in 2002 at the age of seventy-one.

Sabre/Travelocity

In July of 1997 Bob Crandall American Airlines Chairman invited me to join the newly forming board of Sabre Holdings, eighty percent owned by American, Sabre was spun out in a little over a year as a public company. Saber did the reservations processing for American Airlines and many other airlines. Travelocity was a Sabre subsidiary. I retired from the Sabre board in 2006 at the age of seventy-four.

CHAPTER 5

Family Matters

As I was reviewing my business career and attempting to identify where good fortune (and perhaps God's blessings) had intervened, it became obvious that the Lord had blessed my family life with good fortune as well. As my sons were growing up, we took our vacations together as a family. As they grew into adults, we continued to spend time together in activities we all loved and enjoyed. For me, it was a respite from my work life and a chance to enjoy my family in ways that were both relaxing and stimulating. I am not sure Barbara would agree that it was good fortune to be dragged into sailing the ocean and skiing in the Rockies, but she was always there with us making the best of things and enjoying herself.

So, my story would be incomplete without briefly mentioning the most significant of these "family matters": sports activities like sailing and skiing; helping my sons create their own business; caring for my wife as she suffered from Alzheimer's; and realizing I had a new partner in my life. The result of spending so much time together was a cohesive family that enjoyed and loved one another.

Family Blessings From Sailing

Cruising the Caribbean

We set out to have an adventure in 1969 and chartered a small sailboat in the British Virgin Islands. We had such an enjoyable time that we came back the following year. In the third year, we invested in a sailboat that would be chartered to others but we could come and use it when we wanted. It turned out to be a good investment. These two or three-week summer vacations continued for seventeen years. These were weeks the family was together full-time, enjoying shared activities: sailing, cooking, swimming, exploring, talking, and even reading. After dinner the family had time for extended discussions on life's issues. It became dark at about seven in the evening in the Caribbean and my wife and I would curl up on our bunks and read. The boys would get bored and ended up reading our books. These discussions and books were an important supplement to the rather mediocre education they were receiving in the California schools.

Over those seventeen years we sailed from one end of the islands to the other visiting every one of the Windward Islands and the Virgins more than once. These islands were incredibly beautiful and were surrounded by coral reefs that teamed with colorful fish.

Sailboat racing

In the early '80s, we bought a boat in California to sail on the Pacific Coast. It did not take long before we got into racing. Initially, the crew was made up of my sons and a few of their friends. As our skill increased we bought a larger, more competitive sailboat. We needed more crew and added more young friends. As our skill increased, we were graced with two mentors: a high school friend of Barbara's, Clark Reynolds, and Jack Sutphen. Clark's business was inventing things for sailing. He had sailed and raced extensively and introduced us to Jack, a world-class sailor of great renown. Jack adopted us and sailed with us for many years. With his help, the skills of our family-centered team grew strongly. At this point, we looked for an even better boat and found one built right in our own back yard in Santa Cruz, California. At fifty-two feet, it was roughly the same size as the one we intended to replace, but was much lighter and faster. It was better for both racing and cruising.

When I went to order a Santa Cruz 52, I learned the company had just gone out of business. So, for not very much money, I bought the company and had our boat built. We loved it. The boat was named "Elyxir" after our previous boats

At this point my sons and I decided to see if we could sell some more boats and keep the company going. We named the company Santa Cruz Yachts. In fact, we did sell, twenty-one more boats over the next eight years. In 2004, I sold the company to the man who had been the production manager when I bought the company. He had eventually invested some money and become our partner.

Over the twenty years we had raced all over the Pacific Coast from San Francisco to Puerto Vallarta, Mexico. We had cruised up and down the coast more than a dozen times. About 2005, I had to give up competitive sailing because of issues in both legs and my back. Son Skip is now the skipper and continues to race as much as possible. Skip raced *Elyxir* to Hawaii a few years ago and had a fabulous time. He came in second and created many wonderful memories

Good Fortune 51: Ely family blessings from sailing.

What a blessing. Sailing molded our family together; it easily could have done the opposite. The power of the wind and waves is awe-inspiring. Sailing on the open ocean brings one close to the wonders and beauty of God's creation, as did the beauty of the Caribbean islands and the California coast.

Family Reunited Through Skiing

The family started skiing originally in the Sierras, but then we discovered Colorado and, in particular, Vail. We started going to Vail for skiing over the Christmas holidays and after a couple years invited my sister, her husband, and two children to join us. We hardly knew one another, since she was only eleven when I left home. They loved it and returned the next year from their home in Ohio (not renowned for its great skiing). We have been having family Christmas together there since the mid-seventies. In 1980 I bought a condo across from Vail's first gondola for the family to share. As the family grew over the next ten years, I used our building's right of first refusal to end up with two units next to one another with great location and views. These adjacent third floor units were back-to-back and I was then able to combine them to create a six-bedroom condo with a large living area.

We would often have twelve family and friends skiing together. During the day, we enjoyed the fresh air, exhilarating physical activity and the grandeur of the Colorado Rockies. In the evenings, we cooked, ate our meals together amidst laughter and great camaraderie. We slept like babies until I ordered everyone up for another day of skiing. After dinner, we would share our views on current events and our philosophy of life that led sometimes to wonderful, if heated, discussions. It was reminiscent of my discussions with Dad when we were growing up. Our sons and my sister's children have become great friends and, together with their spouses and our six mutual grandchildren, carry on the tradition of the holidays in Vail.

Good Fortune 52: Reunited with sister and family.

Were it not for skiing, it is unlikely that my sister and I, living across the country from each other, would ever have reunited as adults. Skiing brought us together and eventually brought my sister and her family west to live. The cousins became good friends and see each other frequently, even when skiing is not involved.

My Sons – Partners in Business

Shortly before I left Convergent, my sons announced they wanted to start their own company. Both sons were working at 3Com; Glenn as a salesman, and Skip as an engineer. The company offered a sabbatical after six years of employment. They took that plus some vacation time and spent much of the winter in Vail. That's when they decided they wanted to buy a beer distributorship and start their own company. To buy the distributorship, they intended to sell all of their founder's stock and asked me if I would join them as a one-third partner. They had a strategy to take advantage of the coming consolidation in beer distribution and soon found a small Coors distributorship in Santa Cruz that fit their strategy. I agreed to invest with them and to help oversee the acquisition of the others.

They decided to name their business Elyxir Distributing (our sailboat name). As their partner, I helped them put together the deals to carry out the consolidation strategy. I also helped them set up their accounting system and their bank financing. There were five other small family-owned distributors in the three counties surrounding Monterey Bay and it took about ten years to consolidate all of them. When the consolidation was completed, the now large distributorship had less than half the employees and facility space of the five prior companies. As the business grew, we set up a partnership to buy property and build a facility for their expanding business. They have continued to develop the property around them and their real estate partnership is quite successful.

They rarely need my advice or help anymore. They have built a solid company with good employees and excellent financial performance. They have paid off much of the debt it took to put it altogether. Today, as I write this, through gifts and notes they have acquired my interest in both businesses. How fortunate I am to have two sons who love one another and have been my best friends throughout their lives. (Okay, after they turned twenty!) They now give *me* helpful advice. In addition, my sons have blessed me with two outstanding daughters-in-law and four beautiful and talented granddaughters.

Good Fortune 53: *What more could a father hope for!*

My relationship with my sons is a great blessing. We are lifelong, loving friends. It is immensely rewarding to witness their success with their families as well as in their business.

Alzheimer's — It Stole My Wife

You may recall my wife, Barbara, was formally diagnosed with early onset Alzheimer's in 1987. Many symptoms were apparent much earlier. For example, she could not handle the checkbook, nor could she pass her driver's license test. In 1984-85 when she was fifty-three, we saw several doctors and neurologists who investigated brain tumors and other possible causes but found nothing. As this went on, I remained in denial, but that ended in 1987 with the clear diagnosis from an Alzheimer's expert in San Diego.

As the disease progressed, I was faced with a wife who was slowly transforming from the bright-eyed, lovely woman I married into one with vacant eyes and a changed personality. The fact that I also was in my fifties and sixties, and still working, complicated the issues of Barb's care. Geri took on some of the responsibilities of care by doing things like handling the checkbook and doing food shopping. She also was key in helping to find caregivers.

For the first five years Barbara was cared for at home and then in three different facilities, each appropriate for the level of care she needed at the time. With Geri's help I hired many people for Barbara's care but only five were with her for a year or more. Not only did Geri find the caregivers, but she did the payroll as well, which included paying the government taxes and filing all the forms. This was on top of her job with me at my work.

As the disease progressed, Barbara had to be moved to a more comprehensive care facility and eventually, for the last year of her life, a full nursing facility. At each stage of the disease, the kind of caregiver she needed changed. With Geri's help, we found just the right woman at each stage to be with Barbara all day to make sure that every need was met. I would come and see her every day at four p.m. and often sat with her on a lovely shaded patio just outside the sliding door to her room. When I could not be there, which was not often, Geri or another friend would visit with her. During these years, I did not take long trips either for business or for vacations. Barbara avoided most of the bizarre behavior you often hear about with Alzheimer's.

I was truly blessed with the wonderful women who took care of my wife over those years. Eventually, it took more than an hour just to feed her. The care those devoted women showed my wife not only comforted her, but softened my pain as I watched the woman I loved disappear into nothingness day by day.

Barbara passed away peacefully in her sleep on May 30, 2000. We had a short service the next week at the Episcopal Church just across the street from the nursing home. Only my sons and I attended. In the fall, we had a memorial service for her with forty or fifty of her friends. This was a joyful occasion with lots of pictures of the fun we all had shared together. We celebrated Barb's beauty, grace, style, and her wonderful sense of humor with good memories and much laughter.

Good Fortune 54: God-given care for my ailing wife.

It is hard to find any good fortune in losing a wife to Alzheimer's. I do feel that the loving caregivers softened some of the agony. Likewise, the hard-to-understand peace and enjoyment I experienced during my time with Barbara each day was a gift. This continued even when she no longer recognized me nor could talk.

Life Goes On

Now I was alone in a big house that was filled with many memories. I soon sold the house and moved into a townhouse. My loneliness turned my thoughts to Geri. I asked my sons and my sister how they felt about my dating Geri. They indicated that I should go forward with my life. We had a few dates later that winter and spring. It was my sister who helped me move forward. She and her husband were planning a cruise to Alaska and invited me along. And she also suggested I invite Geri. We finalized the group with our dear friends, Jean and Howard Hamilton, from

Florida. Geri was hesitant to go but finally gave in to my pleading. After a few days on the trip we were having so much fun and laughter we all appeared to have been friends for life.

It took time and a lot of soul searching on both of our parts, but Geri and I finally decided to go forward together. I invited her to move in with me. Geri and I were married on September 25, 2000. It has been a blissful relationship ever since. I will never forget the exciting and wonderful years I shared with Barbara, the mother of my sons. But I am so grateful to the Lord for providing a perfect partner for me in my later years, a rock, a lovely spiritual being, and a dear friend—Geri.

Good Fortune 55: The Lord provides.

Geri became my secretary and assistant in 1968. Little did I know at that time the important role she would play in my life for the next forty-five years. Always thinking first of others, her kindness, generosity, joy, and wisdom were gifts from God. I am deeply grateful for her presence in my life.

PART III — AIM

Finding New Purpose and Direction

That morning in April 2008, when I became aware of God's presence in my life, changed everything. Strangely enough I did not doubt what I had been told at the end of that experience. Somehow I knew it was true that my successful life had not been my doing; my wonderful life was God's doing. Talk about a wakeup call!

Now I had something to do; I had been told to "find God." Part III — Aim is the story of where that effort led me. I had always felt there was a God and had accepted He had been present in my life. But as the first step in finding God it seemed appropriate to assure myself that God actually existed. You will see that this path I started on certainly led to new purpose and direction for my life

Chapter 6

My Awakening

As a preface for what followed from that morning, here is that story once again, as told in the introduction. -

Early in the morning on April 15, 2008, I was lying in bed thinking over my plans for the day as I normally do before getting up. This, of course, was tax day and also the day of Pope Benedict's visit, none of which seemed to have anything to do with what happened next. As I lay there, quite suddenly an overwhelming feeling of intense gratitude and thankfulness for the good fortune that had filled my life swept over me. The intensity and depth of this experience is well beyond my limited ability to describe or relate. It continued as I saw my entire life flashing before me like a YouTube video.

I saw my childhood and my wonderful parents who guided me so well in a home filled with laughter and security, in spite of the Great Depression and the Second World War. I relived my undergraduate college days and the fun and friendships balanced with my much-enjoyed but intense studies in engineering physics. I saw my first date with Barbara Sheiry, then our marriage, the start of our life together, the birth of our two sons and my first years as an engineer. Then came the move to California and my years at Hewlett Packard where I learned so much and experienced almost unbelievable success. I started as an R and D engineer and twenty years later, I was an executive vice president responsible for more than half of a multi-billion-dollar company.

I'm not sure how long this "video" took, possibly only seconds, but it was fully detailed. At the end came an amazing realization— **it had been God working in my life who had created my success and life of good fortune**. It was not my skill, capability, or initiative, it had been God. This realization was implanted permanently. I had no doubt. Then I heard the message, *"Paul, you must find God."*

I came down stairs and told Geri what had happened. She looked at me, smiled, and said, "I have been expecting something like this to happen, and now it has." My wife has total trust in the Lord who had provided for her in the struggles bringing up her daughter alone. She prays privately each night before bed and I knew she had been praying for me even before we were married. She never pushed her faith on me but it was clear she was delighted by this event.

To some it might be a downer to discover that a successful career and family were not really due to your own talent and initiative with a little good luck thrown in. For me, this revelation solved the mystery that had for a long time concerned me about why had I so much "good luck" and when would it come to an end? However, now I faced a new mystery. I understood the source of my good fortune was God, but Why Me? Since I had been commanded to find God, it seemed best to do that before trying to answer "Why Me"?

Good Fortune 56: Awakened to God's providence in my life.

What an over whelming revelation this was. Here I was fully re-tired with few responsibilities, a comfortable life, things going well in my family, happy in my second marriage. BAM! I now have tasks to do and more to come. My reaction to this was excitement. I was ready to gain new purpose and direction for my life.

Finding God

God was a total puzzle to me. I suspected there was a God out there some place but that was the extent of my understanding. I had not attended church on any regular basis since I left home to go away to college. I had been told I must find God, so off I went to do that. It seemed the first place to look was probably a church (very clever, Paul). There was an Episcopal church just two blocks from my house, so that Sunday I attended the service there. Geri offered to go with me but I knew she had stopped attending church regularly when her daughter Maria had finished college and had gone off to start her own career; Geri had her own private way of communing with God. The Episcopal Church was what I had attended as a youth with my family. In fact, I had become an acolyte to avoid Sunday school and knew the service well. I enjoyed the local church and several members of the congregation invited me afterwards for coffee with ten or so others. They were very friendly and welcoming but, as I walked home, something told me this was not the place I was meant to be.

A side note: as in most Episcopal churches, the congregation that morning recited the Apostles' Creed. As an acolyte fifty years earlier I must have recited it hundreds of times and was mostly able to do so that morning. Read it below from the Episcopal Book of Common Prayer:

"I BELIEVE IN GOD, THE FATHER ALMIGHTY, CREATOR OF HEAVEN AND EARTH. I BELIEVE IN JESUS CHRIST, HIS ONLY SON, OUR LORD. HE WAS CONCEIVED BY THE POWER OF THE HOLY SPIRIT AND BORN OF THE VIRGIN MARY. HE SUFFERED UNDER PONTIUS PILATE, WAS CRUCIFIED, DIED, AND WAS BURIED. HE DESCENDED TO THE DEAD. ON THE THIRD DAY HE ROSE AGAIN. HE ASCENDED INTO HEAVEN; AND IS SEATED AT THE RIGHT HAND OF THE FATHER. HE WILL COME AGAIN TO JUDGE THE LIVING AND THE DEAD. I BELIEVE

IN THE HOLY SPIRIT, THE HOLY CATHOLIC CHURCH, THE COMMUNION OF SAINTS, THE FORGIVENESS OF SINS, THE RESURRECTION OF THE BODY, AND THE LIFE EVERLASTING." AMEN

I had said the words but did not actually believe. I was not an un-believer but "finding God" meant I had to decide did I believe or not

The next Sunday I choose to attend the Menlo Park church that had been recommended to me many times over the years. As I walked into the sanctuary I heard a wonderful female voice singing a contemporary Christian worship song. The band and the worship music that morning spoke to me. The music was followed by a few announcements and then the sermon. The pastor, John Ortberg, was widely renowned for his sermons. The service was wonderful, no ritual, just worship music and a sermon focused on the Bible (we did recite the Lord's Prayer). I had no question—I belonged in this church.

Inspired by Christian fellowship

I saw in the church bulletin that there was a class on prayer the following Sunday after the service. When I attended and the class finished, a nice gentleman sitting directly behind me introduced himself and asked if he could call me the next day. He said he had something he thought I would enjoy. He did call and invited me to join him at a men's Bible study at seven thirty a.m. the next Saturday.

That men's Bible study was truly an amazing experience, very inspirational and a real eye-opener. Sixty or seventy men attended this class regularly. Some of these men had founded the class more than thirty years earlier. The format of the class is about forty minutes of interactive Bible study conducted by one of the pastors. Often the senior pastor, John Ortberg, would teach and sometimes pastors from other churches would do so. After the lesson was a time for prayer; individuals would stand and request prayer for family, friends, or themselves with health or family problems.

What was so amazing was the behavior, and scriptural knowledge of the men in that room. The pastors loved teaching there. They invited comments or questions during the lessons to solicit insight from the group. The teachers often got as much knowledge as they gave. The prayer requests were deeply moving, sometimes quite sad and often inspiring. The practice of the group was to send a card with appropriate Scripture to each prayer recipient, including a picture of the group and signed by everyone present. These prayer cards were highly valued by those who received them and frequently resulted in heartfelt letters of thanks. Often the thank you would report an answer to our prayer. This impacted me strongly. I felt God working in that room and redoubled my efforts to know and relate to Him.

Overcoming obstacles

The church learning from the sermons and the Bible study continued, but I also started reading books as a key part of my task to find God. Reading the Bible independently of Bible study class was creating very limited understanding of God at this point. I had learned from the church in both the sermons and Bible study classes how important understanding the context and the interpretation/Greek translation was to understanding the meaning of Bible verses. I went on Amazon in search of reading, and before I did anything, up popped *The Shack* by William Young. It was quite new and had shot to the top on the bestseller list. This book was an allegory. It was the story of a man who had experienced the loss of a child and meets God and Jesus as resident characters in a shack in the woods. It was a moving and fascinating story that helped me realize how very little I actually knew about Christianity.

When I finished *The Shack*, I returned to Amazon and, again, immediately presented in front of me was *The Language of God* by Francis Collins. The author, an MD and PhD, was a pioneering medical geneticist who headed the Human Genome Project that succeeded in decoding the human genome. He was an atheist and decided after the genome project to use the scientific method to prove or disprove the existence of God. As a result of this effort, he became a committed Christian. His book wrote of that experience. That book overcame the obstacles created by my life in engineering and science to the supernatural nature of Christianity. Collins showed that there was no conflict between science and the Bible. That book brought me much closer to "finding God."

Collins, in *The Language of God,* made frequent reference to *Mere Christianity* by C.S. Lewis, so that was my next book. Wow—a wonderful book that was extremely helpful. First, Lewis' writing style truly captivated me. His creative use of examples to enhance understanding played to my technical nature. His no-holds-barred style in describing the demands of Christianity struck home. Many more of his books have provided insight and enjoyment for me since that first experience.

My wife and I loved Hawaii. We acquired a condo on Maui in 2001. We managed to go there three or four times a year and stay six or seven weeks each time. When we went in the summer of 2008, I needed to find a good "Bible teaching, Jesus believing" church there. Our condo was adjacent to a golf course and about four hundred yards down the hill next to the fairway was a three-sided former barn that on Sundays housed a church. We could hear the music from our condo and often when playing golf on Sunday could see the crowd there. So the Sunday after we arrived I decided to walk down and see what it was all about. How fortunate was this? The format and content was much like the service at my church in California, great worship music followed by a Bible-teaching sermon. I attend it faithfully when we are there on Maui. The church there has grown and now has more than four hundred members.

Reading continued at a good pace throughout the remaining months of 2008. I read several books by John Ortberg. I came across Francine Rivers—a very interesting author. Her trilogy, *The Mark of the Lion,* is a fictional story of a young Christian girl captured by the Romans in 70 AD when Jerusalem was destroyed. Her story as a slave in Rome and later, Ephesus, was woven around the early church. As I acquired books to read, Geri read them also so we could discuss them.

The search ends

At Christmas 2008 my sister gave me the book *Loving Monday* by John Beckett, a well-known Christian businessman. John was a friend of my sister. This book strongly connected with me. John was an engineering graduate from MIT who had worked in the aerospace industry until his father asked him to come join his small eleven-employee manufacturing company. Not long after he had done so, his father died suddenly and then a fire destroyed much of the company facility. In this crisis John turned to the Lord for help and gave his life to Jesus. As the company grew he decided he could not leave his faith home on Sunday and brought it in on Monday to guide his business life. These Christian principles caused him to establish a company culture much like I had experienced at Hewlett Packard. This realization seemed very important to me, all the more so because neither Bill nor Dave overtly spoke of their faith. I wanted to learn more about John Beckett.

Then I discovered on the inside back page of John's book my sister had written the web address for a site authored by John (Life'sGreatestQuestion.com). It started with a brief summary of how John came to the Lord, then several pages which outlined the Christian Gospel in John's own words. John's words were very persuasive. At the end a brief prayer was offered:

"Jesus, I need you. I repent for the life I've lived apart from you. Thank you for dying on the cross to take the penalty for my sins. I believe you are God's Son and I now receive you as my Lord and Savior. I commit my life to follow you."

When confronted with the prayer, strong emotions welled up in me. I slowly prayed the prayer with tears streaming down my cheeks. This was a very emotional event. It was early February 2009.

Good Fortune 57: The first step on a long road.

I had found God but soon realized the next step was to know God. It had taken nine months to reach this point, but the road ahead was much more arduous. Thinking back, now I realize it was not the hope of eternal life that motivated me at that point. It was my aim to follow Jesus so I could become like the men in that room at men's Bible study. Most of the men whose faith and knowledge I so admired had become Christians in their youth and had studied the Bible in Christian fellowship for dozens of years. I was guided to start this journey with daily Bible reading and prayer. Fellowship with other Christians is a foundation of the faith. It has grown as an important activity for me.

Beginning a New Christian Life

After my decision to follow Jesus, I stared at that prayer page for quite some time. Then I noticed at the bottom of the page was the copyright of an organization, Global Media Outreach. That name startled me. I had heard it a little more than a month before. Our pastor, John Ortberg, had sat next to an interesting gentleman on a flight. Ortberg, who was scheduled to teach at the men's Bible study the following Saturday, was so impressed he asked the individual to take his place and tell his story. The gentleman was Walt Wilson, the founder of Global Media Outreach.

Walt told us how his experiences in the marines had brought him to the Lord. He went on to explain that after an exciting career in Silicon Valley, including time at Apple with Steve Jobs, he had founded Global Medal Outreach. He explained the goal of this organization was to present the Gospel to everyone in the world more than once by the year 2020. Wow, what a bold man with a fantastic goal. In today's lingo, I was blown away. Was it a coincidence that I was soon to be guided to the Lord on a website written by John Beckett but produced by Global Media Outreach (GMO)?

I was anxious to meet John Beckett, whose book and website had been so important to me. Through my sister, I got John's phone number and was able to have a conversation with him. We agreed to get together that summer (2009) in the Colorado Mountains where he had a home near our condo. We had a wonderful evening together and instantly became friends. At the end of the evening, he told me of a conference GMO was holding that fall in Chicago. He was scheduled to speak and asked if I would be willing to come and tell my story. A few weeks later, John introduced me by phone to Mark Weimer, the president of GMO, who formally invited me to Chicago as a speaker. I agreed to go that fall.

Give prayer a try

Right after my commitment of faith and trust in the Lord, I also committed to daily Bible reading and prayer. I subscribed to a plan for reading the Old and New Testaments in a year. This was pretty heavy going. It covered most, but not all, of the Old Testament and all of the New Testament. I found some very good Bible commentary to help.

My earlier Bible study taught me that when you place your faith and trust in the Lord, you receive the Holy Spirit to guide you; each morning I prayed to be filled with God's Holy Spirit. In fact, the following January, the church in Hawaii offered immersion baptism in the Pacific. When your head is immersed under the water it symbolizes the death of your worldly self and when you rise out of the water it signifies your new life in Jesus. Thus you are born again!

That first summer my newfound faith brought great regret that my two sons had not been raised in the church as Christians. Their mother and I had both been brought up as Episcopalians; you already know that I had stopped attending regularly once I left home for college. When we first married we lived on Long Island, New York. We were so busy having children and getting a career started we did not even attempt to find a church. Then, when we moved to Florida, Glenn was six months old, and Skip was four: we really slipped up. We were there almost five years and had many friends who were churchgoers; our closest friends had children of similar age. They went to a Congregational church. We should have gone with them. Instead, because we had been brought up as Episcopalians, we tried several Episcopal churches, none of which we were satisfied with. These were bad choices. We tried to find a church again when we first moved to California, but the Episcopal churches in the Palo Alto area during the '60s were far too liberal for either my wife or me.

So my sons had grown up without meaningful exposure to church. Now in the summer of 2009, their father was keenly aware of the magnitude of his failure. My sons were in their early fifties at that time. They knew my story and my concern for them and their families. Serious prayer was still quite new to me, but asking for God's help seemed the only real alternative. So I prayed earnestly and repeatedly that my sons, their wives, and my granddaughters would be drawn to the Lord. My conversion had encouraged them. By 2010 with persistent prayer and very little urging they had started to attend church. My oldest granddaughter was the first to be drawn to faith and became an example to her parents, then her sister and cousins.

Good Fortune 58: Praise the Lord for answered prayer.

Today, several years later, my four granddaughters (two from each son) are in a wonderful Christian school, the families are attending church—full faith is on the way. Prayer works and I soon had other examples of answered prayer.

Guided to Global Media Outreach

That fall, I went to the GMO meeting. What an eye opener. I met many members of the GMO team. Mark Weimer and I got to know one another and started to develop a friendship. Walt Wilson, as chairman, gave a talk outlining their accomplishments in 2009 and their plans for 2010. I particularly enjoyed the many large screen displays on the walls around the room. Several displayed, by location, icons denoting a sampling of individuals all around the world as they viewed the Gospel presentation. The icon changed color for an individual who indicated a decision to follow Jesus. Very impressive!

The presentations were quite interesting. One presentation described the team of volunteer "online missionaries" (OMs) who

141

are trained and vetted to guide the first steps of the individuals who indicate decisions for the Lord. At the time of the meeting there were about four thousand OMs. Walt Wilson gave an excellent presentation that outlined why he was confident that GMO could bring the Gospel to everyone in the world by 2020.

That evening, John Beckett spoke, and at the end of his presentation, he introduced me and described how he had met me. I started my talk by noting that during my business career I had spoken many times to large groups, but this was the first time I was speaking to an audience that knew more about the topic than I did. I told my story of that morning when I had learned of God's presence in my life. I told of the events that had culminated in my commitment to the Lord through John Beckett's GMO website. I ended by stating I now had two goals: one, striving to become mature in my faith; and two, discovering and carrying out God's will for my life.

After dinner that evening, Mark Weimer engaged me in conversation and invited me to come help him at GMO. Flying home from Chicago after the meeting, Mark's invitation to become involved at GMO was on my mind. There were a chain of coincidences leading me toward GMO: Walt Wilson's speech to the men's Bible study, then my sister's friendship with John Beckett whose book and website inspired my decision to follow Jesus, Beckett's long association with GMO, and finally, Mark Weimer's invitation. By the time the plane landed, I had decided that I should at least explore how I might be able to help GMO.

In about a week, I visited Mark at the GMO office, which at that point was located about thirty minutes from my home. He introduced me to the GMO people I had not met in Chicago. Working with such a dedicated team of Christians who, although young in years were mature in their faith, was attractive to me. Mark discussed a couple of projects that needed attention and asked me to consider them.

Working with Global Media Outreach

Mark and I had become close friends. He offered to meet me Monday mornings for breakfast at seven thirty a.m. to discuss my progress in reading the Bible and learning to walk with the Lord. We continued these meeting for several years. I am highly indebted to Mark for his efforts to help me toward my goal of becoming mature in my faith.

For the almost four years that I have been working with GMO the company has grown successfully. Under Mark's guidance, I have had the opportunity to suggest programs and strategies to help GMO achieve its goal of bringing the Gospel to everyone in the world by 2020. I have been able to participate in key projects with many members of the GMO team.

Change at GMO

In late 2012, Mark decided to leave as president of GMO to join with his son and daughter in establishing a new evangelical organization focused on "crowd sourcing" and social media. I will miss Mark and wish him well in his new endeavor.

After Mark left, it seemed appropriate to reconsider my role at GMO. It was pretty obvious to me that I had been guided to GMO. Not only had Mark left, but also the main office was moving to Dallas from Silicon Valley. It would be much more difficult to work with the now-expanded project teams. So I prayed about the situation, looking for guidance.

Meanwhile, it was quite a challenge to replace Mark. Walt made the right decision by appointing an outstanding young man (everyone's young to me) to manage the operations. His name is Nick Runyon. He would be in Dallas and was going to need help in taking on such a large responsibility.

Then it struck me...my unique experiences were management and organizational skills acquired at Hewlett Packard. Over a twenty-year period I had learned and practiced managing and organizing as taught at HP—The HP Way. I had learned from my peers, from my supervisors, and from Dave Packard and Bill Hewlett when both were actively leading the company. I had performed at every management level from engineering project leader to executive vice president. I had success managing an organization widely recognized at the time for its excellence in management. Also at that time, it was one of the most admired companies in the U.S. This was the training the Lord had provided me. Was this what the Lord wanted me to do, to help Nick Runyon learn and succeed in his role leading GMO?

Well, for starters, that would depend on Nick. Did he want a "coach?" Would he be comfortable with me in that role?

Nick and I had planned a call that same week to cover several topics. I decided to present my thoughts in how I might help Nick. As the topic unfolded, Nick was silent. Had I goofed? So I made clear that I understood that "it took two to tango" and if he did not want that kind of help, it was not a problem and I would continue working on the projects as I had been.

Nick ended his silence by stating that, in fact, he had been considering hiring a management trainer. He said he had interviewed someone but when he realized this individual had no successful leadership experience he chose to not go forward. He went on to say that he had been pondering if it was appropriate to talk to me to see if I might be interested in something like that. Consider this string of "coincidences"—when God is active in your life there are no coincidences. Nick concluded that we should schedule a time to meet each week by phone or videoconference and see how it went. It was amazing how my open-ended question had resolved itself.

Where next?

I am not sure what the Lord's plan is for me, longer term. Coaching Nick is not a long-term task—he is a quick study and very capable. But I know if Jesus is the focus and center of my life His will and plan will be revealed to me.

For now it is an honor to be involved in GMO. The organization's success in presenting the Gospel has been truly astounding and the conversion rate is equally astounding. We expect 300 million people will view the Gospel on our sites in 2013, and plan on 400 million next year. In fact our *hope* for 2014 is to reach a half-billion people.

One in ten who see our Gospel presentations indicate a decision for Jesus. This is an amazing ratio! Most organizations presenting things on the web are pleased with one or two percent.

In October 2013 we presented for the first time an invitation on a digital billboard in Times Square, New York. It is visible sixteen hours a day through New Year's.

From all over the world, millions are turning to the Lord through GMO—you can see why I am honored to be involved with this organization. GMO's results could only be possible with God's help.

CHAPTER 7

Aim for Eternity

In parallel with my involvement at Global Media Outreach, my journey to become a new person in Christ continued. Reading and studying the Bible expanded, as did my knowledge. I enjoyed my Morning Prayer time and learned to listen for God's still, small voice. I continued reading books about Christian faith. As a result of this, my understanding of eternal life and heaven expanded to help deepen my faith.

Growth Through Fellowship

While in Hawaii in 2010 I joined a men's Bible study organized by Kumulani Chapel, my church there. It is a very diverse group and much younger than the group in California (the oldest is ten to fifteen years younger than me). The teaching each week is done by one of the attendees; several are pastors. A few others are recovered addicts with prison experience. All are very knowledgeable Christians. The size and format fosters a great deal of interaction, which greatly enhances my learning. I highly value the fellowship in this group

Something similar has come about in the Bible study group in California that was so helpful in inspiring me as my journey started. Since 2011, I have been part of a group of ten or so men who share breakfast together after the Saturday morning meeting. The breakfast again leads to lots of interaction and fellowship on the morning lesson, and frequently other topics. You will recall the California group that meets Saturday mornings is much larger, sixty or seventy older men.

In 2013, I have found a wonderful new opportunity to grow as a Christian. A Christian friend from the breakfast group above, after repeated attempts, persuaded me to attend Bible Study Fellowship (BSF) meetings weekly in the evening at our church. More than two hundred people from churches all over the local area attend. BSF has thousands of such groups all over the world. The content and the format of the studies are very effective and the same everywhere.

Each week there is a daily assignment of reading and questions. In the evening meeting we first spend an hour, interacting in fifteen-person small groups to discuss that week's reading and answers to the questions. Then all the groups gather to hear a forty-five-minute lecture on the past week's lesson. As we leave we are given an excellent written commentary on that lesson plus the next week's daily assignments. BSF starts in September and finishes in May, covering one book of the Bible. This is a true in-depth learning experience and the small groups provide fellowship.

I now am growing and learning in three different fellowship groups. The men in each of these groups differ greatly from one another. I can learn something from every one of them.

Growth Through Writing

The insights about my life that have come to me in the process of writing this book are amazing. Perhaps it should not be so amazing, because I have been re-examining my life not so much in terms of what I was doing, but in terms of what God was doing.

Writing this book has become so much more than it started out to be. I have gained important new insight into the events of my life by going back and looking at those events with the perspective of my new life with Christ. A draft of the book had been written before my new perspective was fully formed. Here is what I said in the Introduction.

The next step was to go back over the story and identify where there were providential events.... Identifying these providential events by their nature was quite subjective. In a few instances there was no question that something very unusual and quite difficult to explain was going on. While I was going back over the draft identifying these events, often I came to a new and deeper understanding of my life experiences. These providential events are marked and/or commented on in the book (see list of such events with page numbers in the Caption Table at the end of the book).

So I did that, searching for where providence had intervened in my life and career, I went back through the entire draft. You will have seen throughout what you have read certain text captioned *Good Fortune xx.* In some cases, comments are inserted below the caption. You know from what you have read that more than fifty good fortune events have been identified. Some of these events might have been called good luck at the time but so many events in sequence make it hard to believe they could have happened without providential help. Most people would have been happy to have a few such events: three, four, even five but dozens and dozens? Please checkout the Table of Captions.

In identifying these *Good Fortune* events, a few were also seen as "Defining Moments" which impacted my life for years to come. These moments shaped my path and direction, my values, my personality, and echoed throughout my life.

A few of the events were not normal at all; a three-year visit of Jiminy Cricket on my shoulder or receiving several paragraphs of information when only a couple sentences had been uttered. The pace of my promotions was itself very unusual.

I found providence not just in my career but in my family life and also in dealing with Barbara's Alzheimer's.

One of the most important new insights came as I read back over my departure from HP. Suddenly I realized it had not been God's plan for me to leave HP. He had started to train me to be humble and patient. The next five years in a far less visible and powerful position would have required big changes in my self-image and much patience. This training had barely gotten started when I bugged out on lessons I surely needed. At the time, something told me to stay, but I left anyway. How insensitive I was to all that was happening around me. I should have awoken much earlier to God's presence in my life. He was patient, but finally had to give me a gentle knock on the head that morning in 2008 (I deserved more of a hard smack).

Final Thoughts

It is now 2013. It's been more than five years since that morning when I was awakened to God's presence in my life. I am learning to rely on the Holy Spirit to guide my behavior and help me interpret the Bible as I read each morning. He is teaching me to subdue my pride and surrender myself fully to the Lord. It brings peace and joy to perceive His will and act on it. All are "works in progress."

My time spent helping GMO is immensely rewarding. Knowing that GMO's programs are bringing millions of people to the Lord every month is doing the Lord's work. Hearing the gratitude these new believers express in their messages tugs at my heartstrings, sometimes in sadness but often in joy. To have any role in such an enterprise is a great honor.

My understanding of Christian faith has grown significantly. The start for me was to understand that there was a God who had created the universe and everything in it. The more I have studied the Bible the fact that it is truth becomes self-evident. Each set of verses verifies and supports other parts. There is a web of cross justification across the Old and New Testaments. The Old Testament has many prophecies that have proven accurate across thousands of years. There are more than three hundred prophecies relating to the Messiah, all of which have come true in Jesus and have accurately predicted His life. Wow, quite a record.

A pillar of Christianity is stated in John 3:16: *"For God so loved the world that he gave his one and only Son that whoever believes in him shall not perish but have eternal life."* As a Christian you must believe in the resurrection of Jesus, you must believe in eternal life, you must believe in heaven and hell. My friends in Silicon Valley would call these things and many other Biblical truths foolishness. It was important for me to reconcile my life in science and technology with these basic Christian beliefs.

151

Here is my reconciliation. First of all, if God created the universe, it seems obvious that He lives outside our universe, and where He lives is not ruled by time and space as we are. This realization was a great help in leading me to faith. As the evangelist Greg Laurie likes to say, God is omnipotent, omnipresent, and omniscient. Someone who had the power and knowledge to create our universe also could create another place, another universe, called heaven, where God lives. A place that has other dimensions; a place that does not have space and time.

This "other place" is consistent with the discoveries of scientists studying the universe and its origins. Many have predicted the possibility of parallel universes and their existence based on their research findings.

Others may not find the above rationale helpful or necessary but it freed me to fully comprehend that there is eternal life and I will spend eternity with Jesus and God our Father in a heavenly paradise. This was an important step in building my faith. It took some time; I pledged to follow Jesus in early 2009 and had confessed my sins and repented; I was re-baptized in 2011 by immersion in the Pacific by my pastor in Hawaii. This baptism symbolizes the death of my old life and the birth of a new life in Christ. At each step along the way, my gratitude and love for God grew. I continue in the joy of studying God's Word.

We are body and soul, the body decays and dies but the soul lives on. If we have faith in Jesus, He brings us to that place where He lives with God. He provides new bodies similar to our worldly bodies, but which are perfect. These bodies never decay or age because that place, heaven, has no time dimension. If we do not believe, we do not go to heaven. We are judged by Jesus and then sent to our just deserts in Hades or Hell or the Lake of Fire.

I was told of a bumper sticker that reads:

IF YOU LIVE LIKE THERE IS NO GOD
YOU BETTER BE RIGHT

Here is the problem: you either have faith in Jesus and commit to follow Him, or you don't. You are either for Him or against Him. There is no middle ground. There is no half-saved. The Bible quotes Jesus: *"I am the way and the truth and the life. No one comes to the Father except through me"* John 14: 6.

In the introduction to Part III, Aim, I noted some questions that had wedged their way into my consciousness. Does God have a plan for me? The answer to that question is yes; God has a plan for every one of us. Was He training me for some task? Probably, and possibly that task involves Global Media Outreach; but even that may be a warm-up for something else.

Writing this book may be part of His plan for me. It certainly has been a learning experience. I have asked myself who might gain something from this story; might successful business executives now retired or nearing retirement be encouraged to open their mind to the existence of a God and start exploring? Perhaps this story will speak to anyone in his or her mature years to say that it is never too late to bring God into your life. All I can say is becoming a follower of Jesus has given new purpose and direction to my life. This is a wonderful thing for an eighty-one-year-old: I feel young again and am excited by the future. How great is that!

The individuals who worked with me at HP, or who knew of me may read this book. Most will think I have lost my mind. Of course, as is generally true in northern California, they will think my faith is pure foolishness. But possibly this story of God's grace pouring out a life full of blessings on someone they know might encourage them to look a little further.

Of those questions, the most difficult is why me? I do not know the answer yet and my question remains. Why have I had such an easy ride? Why a life of continuous good fortune and success with barely a ripple of trial or trouble? I only know that life was due to His Providence and am overwhelmed with gratitude and thankfulness. I'd like to end with the following short prayer.

A Prayer of Gratitude and Thankfulness

Born in America to wonderful parents

Parents who provided a worldview that guided my life

Parents who gave me the knowledge to build a family and career

Education at Lehigh and Stanford needed for a career in technology

A wonderful, joyful wife and two sons

Sons who are partners in their own successful business

Sons who remain close to their father in love and companionship

Invaluable learning and character building after being guided to HP

A fantastic career filled with joy, excitement and achievement

Experiences displaying the awesome beauty and power of your creation

An awaking in 2008 to your presence in my life

A gift of the Holy Spirit as I committed to follow your Son, Jesus

A Promise of eternal life with you in heaven

Yes, Lord, I am filled with inexpressible gratitude and thankfulness for this life you have given me

I pray in the Holy name of my Lord and Savior, Jesus Christ.

Amen

Table of Captions

Made in the USA
San Bernardino, CA
15 January 2014